WHEN A FAMILY NEEDS THERAPY

When a Family Needs Therapy

A Practical Assessment Guide for Parents,
Lay Therapists, and Professionals

Gina Ogden and Anne Zevin

Beacon Press : Boston

Copyright © 1976 by Gina Ogden and Anne Zevin

Beacon Press books are published under the auspices of the Unitarian Universalist Association

Published simultaneously in Canada by Fitzhenry & Whiteside Limited, Toronto

All rights reserved

Printed in the United States of America

(hardcover) 9 8 7 6 5 4 3 2 1

The selection from *Knots,* by R. D. Laing, is reprinted by permission of the publisher, Pantheon Books. Copyright © 1970 by R. D. Laing.

Library of Congress Cataloging in Publication Data

Ogden, Gina
  When a family needs therapy.
  Bibliography: p.
  1. Family psychotherapy. I. Zevin, Anne, joint author. II. Title.
RC488.5.O35   362.8′2   76–7750
ISBN 0–8070–2752–9

To our families, past, present, and future

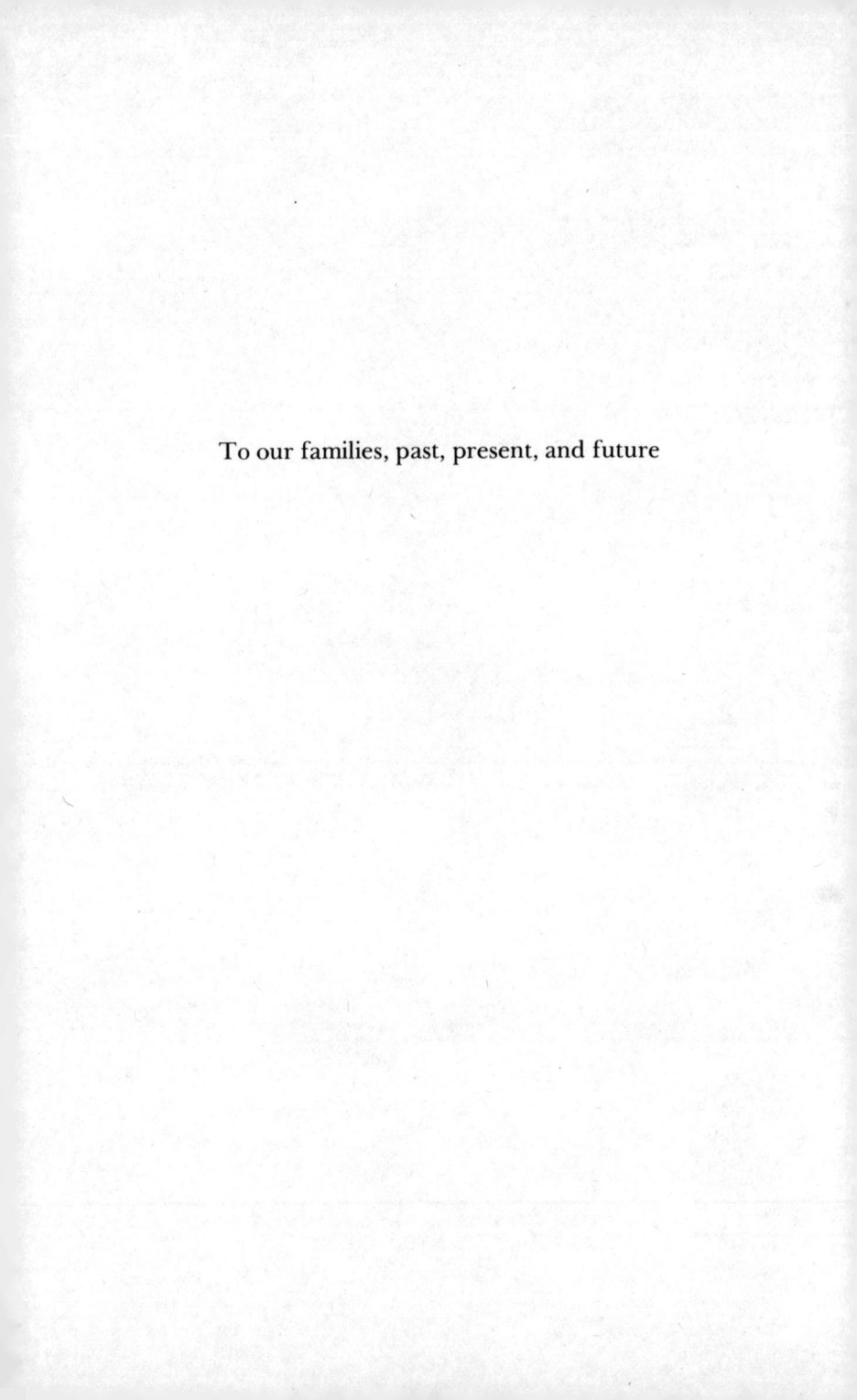

Contents

Introduction ix

1 The Family: Our Definition 1

The family: process, system, mechanisms, dynamics, and skills — being an interviewer: self-awareness; the unobtrusive interviewer; the contract; the tape recorder; small children; co-therapy; interviewing in the family's home

2 Family Skills 13

Communication — problem solving — family self-esteem — receptivity to growth and change

3 Negative Mechanisms 22

"It's impossible" / "I won't play" — general complaining — evasions — denials — double messages — speaking for others — placating — blaming — putdowns — self-putdowns — bribes

4 Family Dynamics 28

Collusions — secrets, myths, taboos — hidden agenda — assumption making — scapegoating — power — boundaries — family alliances — sexism — sharing about sex, money, death, "misfortune" — anger — fear — warmth and emotional support

5 The Interview Kit   36
Skills sheet — negative mechanisms sheet — family dynamics/nonverbal sheet — summary sheet — interview forms

6 Interview I   60
History Taking — Draw a House

7 Interview II   75
Role Card Game — Family Problems — Asking for What You Want — Family Bonanza

8 Deciding Whether You Can Work with a Family   101
Assessing the family — assessing yourself — mutual goals

9 Interview III   104
Interviewer homework — Family Sculpture — feedback — making a contract to work with the family — referring the family

10 Other Uses for the Exercises   116
In family therapy — in group therapy — in crisis prevention — in your own family — in training courses

Appendix 1: Scoring and Numbers   126

Appendix 2: Scoring the Exercises   131

Appendix 3: The Smith Family   165

Bibliography   185

Introduction

When a Family Needs Therapy is a practical assessment guide for parents, beginning or lay therapists, and those professionals considering family therapy as an additional skill. It describes in detail what kinds of things to look for in a family, how to evaluate a family's strengths and weaknesses, and how a lay therapist can decide whether to do therapy with the family h/self or refer to professional therapists.

We feel it is possible to find out the degree to which a family is healthy or not healthy by assessing its Skills in the broad areas of communication, problem solving, family self-esteem, and receptivity to growth and change. In this book we have identified specific Skills in each of these four areas. We describe in detail *three structured interviews* which reveal the measure of each of these Skills. And we provide two evaluation systems: one simple and the other more complex and more accurate. Ironically, it is far easier for clinicians to say in what ways families are not healthy, since that is how they present themselves.

Finally, we present what we have learned about interviewing and evaluating families in a way that will enable others to do a better job, particularly those lay therapists — doctors, lawyers, teachers, guidance counselors, social workers, clergy — who are called on continually for help but do not have the kind of training to make a sound decision whether to help or to refer. What often happens is that the lay therapist finds h/self biting off more than he/she can chew. The therapy fails, and what was meant to be helpful ends in anger, frustration, and even disaster for both therapist and family.

Evaluation of Families: Two Options

Our book is organized to provide you with two evaluation systems, depending on the amount of time and energy you have. First, there is the option of making broad assessments following each exercise. That is, you can tape record the exercises with the family, and then, using the scoring sheets provided in the Interview Kit, write down evaluations either on a numerical scale (we suggest 5–0), or on a descriptive scale (excellent, good, fair, poor, etc.). Or you may choose the more exacting system described in the appendixes and, using the directions and charts provided there for each exercise, come out with a more accurate number.

We recommend trying the more complex system at least once or twice, even though it may seem unbearably time-consuming. We feel you will learn a great deal more about how to listen to and observe interactions between people if you submit yourself to the discipline of filling out all the charts. We worked out the exercises and scoring systems by doing complete evaluations on seven families and trial runs on three others. (All of them were middle-class, white, suburban families.) Our results are in the appendix. We found the more complex process invaluable as a training experience for us. In fact, by the time we had finished the seventh family, eight months after we had started the first, we found the system we had devised had strengthened our powers of clinical observation so much that each of our offhand guesses of scores proved to be accurate when we did them the long way.

Language

We've tried to keep the language in this book, like the language we use in therapy, as direct and jargon-free as possible. Where we've needed to use professional terms like "process" and "system," we have defined what we mean in the text as soon as necessary.

The problem of using the pronouns he, she, his, hers, him, her, himself, herself in a way that does not define all people as male is an awkward one which does not lend itself to an elegant solution. We've done our best to be consistent.

The Smith Family

We made up a family for the book, the Smith family — John, Mary, Billy, and Suzy, using one of our healthy families as a baseline, so that when we give examples of scoring, charts, and notes you will have a consistent frame of reference. Where other names are used, it is because the Smith family, even though largely of our invention, would not characteristically contain the examples discussed. (We use a Brown family briefly, pages 28–35, to illustrate troublesome Family Dynamics.)

Acknowledgments

The doing of this book felt like a good thing from the beginning — from the seed-concept of doing some kind of project about families together. And now, two years later, with the galley proofs about to appear, it still feels good. We managed to generate for each other a positive growth-energy throughout the creation of the book and throughout some major changes in each of our lives. We know this kind of energy does not come out of nowhere, and here we would like to acknowledge, with thanks, some of the sources that helped this book grow:

The Goddard College Graduate Program for being liberated enough about education to reward us for undertaking the joint project which became this book;

All the families who opened themselves to us in the interviews on which the book is based;

Our clients who taught us, and are still teaching us, about what it means to be a therapist;

Simone Real, who truly cared about typing the original project with its plethora of charts and tables;

Ray Bentley, our Beacon Press editor, who knew we had written a book;

And our teachers along the way;

Eileen Cooney and Maddy Gerrish, who supervised the original project and much of our training;

Jeremy Cobb, Meredith Kantor, and Robert Ravven, Anne's guides and mentors, and, through Anne, teachers of Gina;

Eleanor Hamilton, who gave us our first clear view of the love path.

WHEN A FAMILY NEEDS THERAPY

Chapter 1
The Family: Our Definition

It is pertinent here to talk about what a family is at a time when there seems to be some doubt that the family means what it used to, or even that it is destined to continue in any recognizable form.

Traditionally, a family is a group of people who are related by blood or marriage, living mostly in the same place, depending on each other in many ways for survival, and having a legal status in the society. Families each have unique styles, traditions, rules, value systems, and methods of operating which differentiate one from the other.

Ideally, the traditional family includes the following elements: *trust,* actively developed and maintained; *commitment* among all members to interrelate, to participate in family decisions and to anticipate the future; *expectation* of needs being met — emotional, physical, intellectual, and economic; *communication* — a sense of responsibility to hear the other members and to share feelings with them; and *shared living space* with free access in and out for everyone.

The family is indeed a support system which, when it works well, is the best basis for human development most people can envision. Unfortunately, even when the family is not operating well as a support system for its members, it remains the most viable place for children to be raised. The alternatives in our society are in most cases worse.

There is a small but growing sense that the family, as we have experienced it, is a dying institution. Also there has been much political debate on the proposition that the family is an oppressive institution in itself and a breeding ground for increasingly authoritarian and oppressive societies.[1] Are we propping up what is at best a dying institution and at worst an evil one?

Newly created socialist societies, such as Israel, China, and Cuba, have for some years been experimenting with changing some of the functions of the family — child-care, housing, financial and medical responsibility — so that currently responsibility for planning and executing those functions rests more on the society as a whole, freeing adults in families for the labor force. While the ideologies of collective socialism are involved, we must remember that the necessity behind these inventions has been to provide a more productive agrarian and industrial work force. Even with these new government policies, however, the family in China, Cuba, and Israel (outside of the kibbutz system) remains much like the family in the West — a primary support system.[2]

In Western nations also, some of these new ideas are being put into operation, particularly national health plans and public higher education. Where child-care has been instituted by government policy, it has been for economic reasons. In the United States, the thrust for child care centers, without which the family cannot change very much, has two main sources: the women's movement, and the Department of Health, Education and Welfare. Plans for child care centers in the United States, however, except in rhetoric, are not on the scale of the kibbutz system in Israel,[3] nor are they likely to become so without a major government effort. Since the United States is not suffering a labor shortage, this kind of an effort seems hardly likely. Therefore, we do not see the family becoming a much changed entity here. While the debates about the family continue, and even while we may participate in those debates, the place where most of us live and where small children will continue to get whatever support

---

[1] David Cooper, *The Death of the Family* (New York: Random House, 1970).
[2] Ruth Sidel, *Women and Childcare in China* (New York: Hill & Wang, 1972).
[3] Bruno Bettleheim, *Children of the Dream* (New York: Avon, 1971).

they are going to get is still the family. We are not proposing that families are the only or the best support systems, or that all families should be held together — only that families are mostly what we have to work with.

There are many smaller changes in the United States and elsewhere, and we see the definition of family as being increasingly open to change in terms of lifestyle. Collective living is becoming increasingly viable,[4] so that a family may no longer mean anything about blood relationships or legal status. Marriage in the legal sense is certainly a questionable goal for many.[5] One-parent families with adopted children are being encouraged in some states. With new abortion laws, babies born out of wedlock are being brought into the world by choice, and are therefore more often kept by the mother than before. Rights of fathers are a more open question in the courts, so that, following divorce, we are seeing more fathers being given custody of children. It seems that families are becoming, more and more, families of choice.

During our clinical training, one of our first tasks was to work out a definition for a family of choice: "A family is two or more people who choose to live together, and who are committed first to their own individual growth and secondly to the individual growth of each other member."[6]

This definition seems to us to have many merits, even for a family which is not all "of choice." (That is to say, children do not have a choice to leave the family very early because they are dependent on the family for support.) We look at this definition as a guideline for goals as we live together in our own families, and certainly as a guideline for any two people who wish to begin a new family. It works, too, when two or more families contemplate living collectively, or when several individuals who are not related biologically wish to live together.

[4] Robert Houriet, *Getting Back Together* (New York: Coward, McCann & Geohegan, 1971).
[5] Nena O'Neill and George O'Neill, *Open Marriage* (New York: M. Evans, 1972).
[6] Maddy Gerrish and Eileen Cooney, from Training Course in Family Process and Therapy, Bedford, Mass., March to July, 1973.

THE FAMILY: PROCESS, SYSTEM, MECHANISMS, DYNAMICS, AND SKILLS

Background. In the mid-fifties, a group of professionals from very different disciplines — including Margaret Mead and Gregory Bateson from anthropology; Ray Birdwhistell from anthropological linguistics; Jay Haley, Don Jackson, Virginia Satir, John Weakland, and others from psychology and psychiatry; and Paul Watzlawick from cybernetics — came together in Palo Alto, California, in an effort to understand the problem which had confounded mental health workers for decades — the problem of schizophrenia. They had at least two common assumptions — that schizophrenia was not an inherited disease, and that it was the result of some kind of block in communication between the schizophrenic and significant others. The result of their work was a comprehensive understanding and defining of the family as a system and a detailed examination of the process of communication between human beings.[7] There were some parallel conclusions made at the same time in Britain by A. Esterson and R. D. Laing, also working to unravel the problem of schizophrenia.[8] Many of the specific conclusions of the Palo Alto group and Laing et al. have been revised and challenged, but the basic view of the family as a system has gained acceptance among a broad base of mental health workers all over the world.

The implications of this view of the family as a system are interesting. There is, for example, the possibility that all intrapsychic work has been irrelevant[9] (a threat which produced a schism within the profession), the possibility that all individual treatment was useless and that the entire family had to be seen at all times[10] (chaos in the offices of therapists), the possibility that

[7] Andrew Ferber, Marilyn Mendelsohn, and Augustus Napier, eds., *The Book of Family Therapy* (Boston: Houghton Mifflin, 1973).

[8] R. D. Laing and A. Esterson, *Sanity, Madness, and the Family* (New York: Basic Books, 1970).

[9] Nathan Ackerman, "The Role of the Family in the Emergence of Child Disorders," *Foundation of Child Psychiatry*, ed. Emanuel Miller (London: Pergamon Press Ltd., 1968).

[10] Carl Whitaker and Janet Burdy, "Family Psychotherapy of a Psychopathic Personality: Must Every Member Change?" *Comprehensive Psychiatry*, vol. 10, no. 5 (September, 1969).

individuals in treatment whose families would not cooperate were therefore untreatable (those very "schizophrenics" we started out with). For most of the professionals, however, the furor died down and psychotherapists worked out their own methods. These ranged from classical Freudian psychoanalysis as a technique (with the current family as a frame of reference and a reality for the patient) to making contracts with families to treat them only and strictly as a system (to see them only all together and only for a certain number of sessions which the therapist decided was the number that system required for treatment). Somewhere in the middle of this continuum is the working mode of most therapists.

Those who call themselves family therapists have mainly in common that they work with individuals as these individuals relate to their families. Some therapists never have other family members physically in the office, some sometimes have some, some always have some, and so on. We call ourselves family therapists. That is, we treat individuals in relationship to their families. We see parts of families, we see families with all members together. We also work intrapsychically when there is deep and abiding trauma, in addition to working with individuals as they are in relationship to their family. We always consider people as part of a family and the family as a system — a very powerful system.

Some therapists do not work well with more than one person at a time. They may still operate as family therapists if their basic reference is to the family as a system, rather than to the intrapsychic model.

In the Bibliography you will find much of the relevant writing by the family systems theorists and therapists whose terms and theories we use.

Family Process. Family process is the sum of all of the interactions of the family. No matter how the family is structured or what its goals are, every family has a process. This process has been created largely by the adults in the family who come together, each with an inherited process, sometimes with wishes to change, and combine to create their current process. When you look with an overview at a family, you see how the family *is*. Even if you have never thought about the family in this way, when you are asked to describe a family that lives down the street, you might say something like, "Oh, they don't seem to be too happy. They never do anything together, the kids are all in trouble, there's a lot of yelling, the place is a wreck," and so on. You would be talking about their process.

Family System. The method a family creates to *be* whatever way it is being, is called their system. The whole family has to cooperate in the system to keep it going. If you look a little closer at that family down the street, you might say, "He drinks all the time and can't keep a job." You are looking at a part of the system. If you keep watching, you might see that whenever he stops drinking, she gets physically ill and takes to her bed. It seems as if he would rather be drunk than have her sick in bed, so he gets drunk again. It seems that she would rather be sick in bed than to have him sober, so when he quits, she gets sick. But both of them are engaged in a system which supports their process, and in their process someone always has to be taken care of, everyone has to be unhappy, there can never be enough money, no one can take any responsibility.

Families come into therapy when the process is a bad one and the pain becomes too great. Their system is not working for them; someone is suffering too much. When therapists can get into their system, into the Mechanisms, Family Dynamics, and Skills, they can perhaps help the family to improve their process.

Mechanisms. Mechanisms are individual repeated behaviors that help make the family system function, or dysfunction. In the family down the street he is self-deprecating (does what we will later call *self-putdowns*), *denies* that he has any financial problems, talks incessantly about irrelevant material whenever you see him, drunk or sober. We list it as *defensive long-talking*. She tells him what to do (*gives orders*), makes *sarcastic remarks* about his general ineptness in all things, mostly in his presence, *speaks for* him when he is standing right there, and *complains* constantly about her lot. She feels definitely one-up on him. He feels appropriately one-down and helpless. All of these Mechanisms which help make this system function to maintain their process, we call Negative Mechanisms because the process is a poor or negative process. These are not the kind of Mechanisms which can contribute to a healthy or positive process. We will be talking more about Negative Mechanisms on pages 22–27.

Family Dynamics. Family Dynamics are forces operating in the family system: patterns of behavior, conscious or subconscious, in which two or more members of the family consistently interrelate, and powerful, prevailing attitudes or emotional climates which the whole family maintains, consciously or subconsciously, as the background for their interrelating.

Dynamics as well as Mechanisms help to keep the family system stable, whether it is functioning for a healthy process, or dysfunctioning for an unhealthy process. We are dealing mainly with dysfunctional Dynamics, with some exceptions. The dysfunctional Family Dynamics in the above family might be: they join in a *collusion* to keep him drinking; they *scapegoat* the oldest boy (perhaps unwittingly); there is a family *taboo* against talking about alcoholism; they maintain among themselves the *myth* "if he didn't drink, we would all be happy." We will be dealing more with Family Dynamics, describing each one on pages 28–35, where there will also be a list of the functional Dynamics.

Skills. Skills are the abilities the family has to work out a good system for the purpose of maintaining a healthy family process. All families have these Skills to some degree. Their Positive Mechanisms and Dynamics are part of those Skills. When the Skills are high, and the process is good, we see more Positive Mechanisms and Family Dynamics. When the Skills are low, and the total process is poor, we see more Negative Mechanisms and Negative Family Dynamics.

We have not scored Positive Mechanisms and Positive Family Dynamics. Instead, we have treated these, and the way they make the system work, as part of Skills. Certainly when we talk of the Skill of straight talking/responding, for example, there are Positive Mechanisms involved. In a family with a healthy process, you can easily see the Positive Dynamic of emotional support at work, which contributes to many Skills. We feel that identifying the positive elements of a healthy system is a task for another study.

Healthy Family System. In brief, a healthy family system will maintain a healthy process; one in which people are committed to their own growth and to the growth of all others, physically, mentally, emotionally, sexually. It will be a family which uses Positive Dynamics and Mechanisms to engender trust, warmth, support, sharing, and freedom. It will have high Skills in areas of communicating, problem solving, family self-esteem, and receptivity to growth and change.

BEING AN INTERVIEWER

Self-Awareness

Since this book is about learning to evaluate families, we ask that you take a good look at your own family of origin so that you can understand your own process. Also, look at your current family, whether it be a nuclear one, a relationship with roommates, a collective, or whomever you consider your family. How does it work? Perhaps you can get someone to do the interviews in this book with your family. Are you in good enough shape to objectively and helpfully evaluate others? Or are there some problems you have yourself that you might unwittingly work out on others? Even if you always limit yourself to evaluation and never contract to counsel other families, there is the danger of making so many mistakes when your own process is not clear to you that the evaluating will be meaningless.[11]

---

[11] Nathan B. Epstein, Vivian Rakoff, and John J. Sigal, "Working Through in Conjoint Family Therapy," *American Journal of Psychotherapy,* vol. 21, no. 4 (October, 1967), pp. 782–790.

The Unobtrusive Interviewer

One of the dilemmas confronting those in the social sciences who use interviewing techniques to gather data is the problem of how much the presence of the interviewer changes the behavior of the interviewees. There seems to be no way to avoid being somewhat influential. All we can say is try to be as neutral and unobtrusive as you can in order to be able to see the family system as accurately as possible. Remember that you are evaluating what is happening, and this is not the time to introduce change.[12]

General Instructions for Interviewing

The Contract. You will want to make a contract with the family that all members will be there for all interviews and that all interviews will be tape-recorded. If your contract is with five people and four show up, make a new appointment and send them all home unless the fifth has really gone to Timbuktu, never to be seen again. You will not know how the whole family operates if someone is not there. If you are seeing a family in therapy, there will be times when it is appropriate to see fewer members, but for evaluation it is not. Make it clear from the first phone contact that all members must come each time. If one person tells you that another will not come, call the other person yourself and tell that person you need him/her to find out what goes on in the family. You may find others are wanting to keep that person away, for whatever their reasons.

The Tape Recorder. We have found that when you explain why the tape recorder is being used, people generally will not go on too long about the dangers of what they say being on tape. You will, of course, assure them that the tapes will be under lock and key and will be erased as soon as you have finished with them. If

---

[12]*See* Alfred C. Kinsey, *Sexual Behavior in the Human Male* (Philadelphia: W. B. Saunders Co., 1948), pp. 35–73, for a discussion on how to interview to elicit honest, complete answers.

they want to listen to them, they may, after you have finished with them. Sit near the machine and do not let small children, large children, or adults "help you." If you give them half a chance, the machine will not work that session. Being firm about it will say something about your being in control.

When you listen to the tape after each interview, have pencil in hand and the necessary forms where you can reach them. Make up duplicates of the sheets in the Interview Kit, taking into account the number of people in the family. Have these and a piece of scrap paper to use to list Negative Mechanisms and make notes to yourself on Family Dynamics within easy reach. You will have to stop, reverse, and start again many times when you first begin to use this system, but it will get easier as you go along.

Small Children. Small children may become a problem. We will talk about ways of handling them in specific exercises. Generally, your standard working equipment can include paper and crayons, a box of miniature toys and blocks, so that very young children will be able to amuse themselves at times when they cannot participate. If chaos ensues, with small children out of control in a family, you will learn something from the ways the family deals or doesn't deal with it. If you work in your office rather than in the family's house, and you have rules about your own things in your space, explain them very firmly and straightforwardly to the child. It is your space.

Co-Therapy. We prefer working as co-therapists with families, as we find most families too complex for one person to deal with.[13] The work two people do in one hour seems to add up to more than two hours' work somehow. And there is the advantage of having a partner to model with you examples of communication or asking or whatever. The co-therapist system in addition includes the advantage of two people for clients to

---

[13] Carl Whitaker, Thomas P. Malone, and John Warkentin, "Multiple Therapy and Psychotherapy," *Progress in Psychotherapy* (New York: Grune & Stratton, 1956); Augustus Napier and Carl Whitaker, "A Conversation About Co-Therapy," *The Book of Family Therapy* (Boston: Houghton Mifflin, 1973).

"side" with; that is, at times you might want to be advocate for one parent (or for a child). This leaves the other therapist to be advocate for another family member. There is, too, a built-in supervision system with two therapists. You will have another objective person whose views of what happens differ from your own, and you will both be forced to work out why you saw it differently, thereby eliminating some of the danger of your own biases creeping in.

We find one of the greatest advantages of working as co-therapists is that for the family there is an opportunity to see two people communicating in a straight way. This may well be the first time such a phenomenon has occurred for them. Modeling constantly in your working relationship the Skills you are advocating to the family will be a way of introducing change into their system. It is therefore incumbent upon the co-therapists that they work on those Skills themselves. The co-therapist relationship is a very important one to the clients, and if you are open and clear, including saying negative feelings to each other when necessary, it will be a helpful model.

We are both women, and the question arises of whether two women (or two men) make a good pair as co-therapists. We have never found any difficulty with clients because one of us is not a man. Usually, one parent will identify with one of us more than the other and that seems sufficient. Male co-therapists to whom we have spoken say the same thing. If there is an antimale bias on the part of female therapists, or an antifemale or male chauvinist bias on the part of male therapists, obviously there is a problem. But the sex of the therapists in and of itself doesn't seem to be a block to progress.

Interviewing in the Family's Home. We conducted all our interviews in the families' homes. We felt the interviews would be less threatening to families, particularly to children, if carried out on their home turf. Also, we felt we would learn more about the families as we saw them interacting at home — how they used their space, was the space set up to be equally comfortable for all members, what did it feel like for us to enter into their space.

Looking back on the interviews, we feel that the real value of seeing the families at home was that all members responded freely to one another, rather than being on good behavior or being uptight and scared as they often are in the first few interviews in an office. While we realize that it may be inconvenient and time-consuming for you to travel to a family, we urge you to think about doing at least one of the interviews in the family's home.

Chapter 2

Family Skills

In the next three chapters we will take a closer look at the three aspects of the family system briefly described earlier — *Skills, Negative Mechanisms,* and *Family Dynamics*. An awareness of what is involved in these areas will help you to do the evaluation interviews that make up the heart of the book.

As we mentioned earlier, *Skills* are the abilities the family has to work out a good system for the purpose of maintaining a healthy family process. We have located these in four areas: *communication, problem solving, family self-esteem,* and *receptivity to growth and change.*

COMMUNICATION

Straight Talking/Responding

Honest and direct verbal statements about facts and feelings.

This Skill is essential to clear communication in families; that is, members who have the Skill are able to say directly what is on their minds, and respond directly to what others say. Straight statements are characterized by their nonequivocal nature; they are neither rambling nor confusing. Their tone is clear, not awkward, guarded, or stuttered. They ring true as if the speaker believes in them. A straight talker is not aiming to defend h/self or to attack or trap others, but is always aiming to contact others, to define his/her own self in terms others can understand.

Listening

Hearing accurately what others say.

Good listening skills require enough openness to hear facts and feelings without distorting them. The person who hears only what he/she wants to hear is not listening to what others say. There are people who simply cannot hear bad news; others who cannot hear good things about themselves; others who filter, interpret, or translate what they hear into patterns, like the businessman to whom everything speaks "money," or the teenage rebel to whom any family plan speaks "entrapment." Good listening also requires an accurate memory of what has been said. The twelve-year-old boy who forgot that his favorite uncle was coming to dinner may have had so many other things bouncing around in his mind that day that there was not enough room for either the fact or the emotional content of the message. "I didn't remember, Mom," may be an honest answer. "I can't get through to him" may be Mother's honest perception. It is important to know, in dealing with families, that good, accurate, full listening can occur only when people are open minded and also ready to hear.

Shared Facts, Meanings, Values

Members sharing information directly with one another; operating out of a common frame of reference and ideology.

Do all family members know the same facts about the family — or is it important for the adults to "protect" the children from knowing about money, sex, or Aunt Minnie's alcohol problem? Does Father see himself as the heroic breadwinner, while the others regard him as a joke? Does Mother believe her teenage children to be good Christians while they are operating their lives out of a steadfast atheism? Where there are no major discrepancies such as these, where all family members are aware of their history and their present life situation, where all agree on a framework of values, and where members' functions in the family carry the same kind of meaning to all, a family has been communicating well together and has laid the groundwork for further good communication.

PROBLEM SOLVING

Risk Taking

Members' ability to confront each other with their wants and problems.

Are members able to say directly what they need from one another, and frankly admit problems to each other when they occur? Or do they wait to be asked, pretend they are without wants, needs, problems; or cringe, immobilized, not daring to risk showing themselves to others? A family which has old injunctions or present threats against individuals' stating their wants or needs (especially wants and needs from one another) cannot face problems, let alone solve them. In one family we interviewed, Mother and Father stated only the most generalized problems, while one of the children, not risking saying it in front of the family, wrote on his card: ". . . I don't remember the time we all ate at the same time and went places together. I think that the last time was in kindergarten or the first grade." Such inability to risk asking for basic needs to be listened to, validated, or fulfilled is a position of real pain.

Openness Intra Family

Members' willingness to share directly positive and negative feelings with each other, including those dealing with crisis, loss, death, fear.

Are members able to contact each other physically — hug or push away as feelings dictate, let each other know how they stand? Are they able to enter fully into conversations about their feelings and each others' feelings? In an open family there is a lot of activity, movement, and contact on both a physical and a conversational level. People reach out to each other, respond in a direct way, make decisions taking feelings into account. A family in which members are closed off from each other seems physically stuck in prescribed positions, their conversation sounds stilted. Negative feelings are seldom expressed, and when they are, they are quickly closeted away — better not to open up a can of worms. Openness intra family is something tangible you can sense, as an outsider to the system. There is a relaxed quality about the way the members treat each other — and how they treat you — and a confidence that everyone has some power and mobility.

Negotiating

Members' ability to talk straight, listen, respond clearly, and compromise when necessary.

Negotiating is at least a two-person process involving statements of want/need from each person, listening and responses, the ability to recognize a logistical or emotional impasse when it happens, and the willingness to give up some territory when necessary for the common good. When any of these elements is missing, negotiating is not happening. Members may jump up and down yelling clearly for what they want, but not listening to others. Mother may listen to all, but never state her own needs, then collapse with a headache. Son may never respond clearly to Father's negotiating to get help mowing the lawn — Son feels ordered around, Father feels unheard, and the lawn goes unmowed. Husband and wife may reach an impasse and be unable to make compromises. He: "I want to go away for a weekend together." She: "We can't possibly leave the children." If the feelings behind each of these statements are aired, explored, the negotiating is successful and compromise is possible. Perhaps "I want to go away for a weekend together" simply means "I need to talk to you alone." Perhaps "We can't possibly leave the children" means "I'm afraid they're coming down with strep."

Negotiating is a real working out together of what will make everybody feel O.K.

Decision Making

Members' ability to come to an amicable agreement about common activities within a workable time limit.

Some families, or individuals within families, feel that they can never be satisfied, and so put off making decisions. They either prolong the negotiating process ad infinitum, or openly rebel against any decisions that others make. One of our families added a new twist. The daughter railroaded a decision through about how her family was supposed to spend money, then complained when they went along with her decision. She didn't really want to spend the money on that, she pouted. Family ability to make amicable decisions is essential to problem solving. The degree of ability in this Skill is a critical index of the quality of the family's process. When the process is a good one, both the logistics and the emotional content of the decisions satisfy all members.

Responsibility

Appropriate adult sharing of jobs and functions as parents; teaching children how to grow up as functional adults.

What we mean by responsibility is a willingness to pull your own weight in the family and teach children to grow up to do the same. The overresponsible parent who shoulders all financial and child care duties, who allows the children to drop popsicles on the livingroom rug, and lends a drunken uncle the family car is, we feel, creating a thoroughly irresponsible family system. It is every individual's need to be able to be responsible for h/self. Children can learn this kind of responsibility only from parents who are willing to share jobs and parenting wherever possible, who are not into playing either suffering martyr or controlling dictator. There are families in which there are no responsible adults. The result is chaos, and very often a child ends up with the parent role, seeing that meals are on the table and caring for young children. This insidious role reversal where parents play children and children play parents gets into real pathology and is not within the scope of this study.

FAMILY SELF-ESTEEM

Positive Contact with Each Other

Verbal and nonverbal validating, comforting, caring, directly showing warmth.

Can family members reach out to one another in a giving way? Some families are physically oriented — there is a lot of touching, patting, and hugging. Other families may achieve the same quality of closeness through eye contact, warm tone of voice, and an impeccable timing about when to say what to whom, or when to shut up. It is necessary to notice these kinds of positive contact in a family in order to evaluate their problems and know how to treat them. One of the families we interviewed, in a crisis of family fear and anger over teenage daughter's acting out, showed a marked amount of positive physical contact with each other. The caring between all family members was evident. We knew, therefore, that one way to reduce their anxiety level was to reinforce for them the amount of caring they had displayed to us, and to help them feel good about themselves again.

Ability to Play

Members' enjoyment of each other, their dreams, and fantasies.

Does a family have any fun together, or does it only come together in times of work or crisis? Families in which the members can really enjoy one another's dreams and fantasies are showing a trust that the child within each person is "O.K."[1] This kind of playing ability is not to be confused with the collusive fantasizing that goes on in disturbed families, where the fantasies are only an escape from pain. Families who play well exhibit a confidence and enthusiasm about doing things together: vacations, eating dinner, doing creative projects, playing with words.

Ability to Get What You Want

Family system's success in satisfying the practical and emotional wishes and needs of all members.

In an ideal family everybody is validated and feels good about h/self. The system is set up to encourage members to let their wants be known with a reasonable chance of their being met. But there are family systems which satisfy the needs of only some members, or none. For example, a family who dumps all of its anger onto its scapegoat, keeping the other members feeling validated if only by comparison; or a family stuck emotionally in a devastating past — all members conclude that the future will be like the past, that nobody can ever get what they want.

RECEPTIVITY TO GROWTH AND CHANGE

Accepting Individual Differences

Family permission for each member to develop in his/her own way.

Are members allowed to follow their own unique inner senses of style, taste, timing, and space? Or must everyone follow prescribed personality patterns? "Everyone in our family is musical/unmusical, fat/skinny, neat/messy, outgoing/shy . . ." In some families these injunctions are so strong that members obey them for life; if a member of such a family behaves differently, he/she ceases to belong to that family; becomes an outcast, a black sheep, a maverick. In families where individual differences are accepted, however, the rules are different: each member is encouraged to try out kinds of behavior that work best for him/

---

[1] Thomas A. Harris, *I'm OK, You're OK* (New York: Harper & Row, 1969).

her — to develop special talents, explore ideas and personal relationships — without risk of being blackballed from family membership.

Limit Setting

Members' ability to describe boundaries to maintain privacy, protection, functioning, and self-definition.

A family that can set no limits — in which all members act out all their whims all the time — may seem very creative at first glance, but is in fact hamstringing itself. How can members have privacy when they need it if all rooms are common property; how can members protect themselves from aggression if nobody is allowed to say "stop"; how can members function and grow when they are continually distracted by others; how can members say, "This is who I am," if "I" has no boundaries? This describes a pathological family. What we mostly saw in our interviews were families in which one member was unable to describe self-boundaries — felt walked over by others — or in which one member was allowed to distract and interrupt others. Limit setting requires first that you know where you end and other people begin, and then the ability to state this boundary clearly so that others can hear it. "No" is a good boundary enforcer. So are "not now" and "that's enough." People who are able to set reasonable limits are freer to grow than those who aren't. Families in which all members are able to set limits when they need to have a much more open quality.

Internally Chosen Roles

Free, conscious, nonstereotyped decisions by each member of how he/she will function as an individual within the family system.

We refer here especially to sex and age roles. Are men, only, expected to earn money and repair the car; women, only, expected to do housework; children expected to do only as they are told. In such a family it can become a crisis if mother takes a job or daughter enters business school. And what if father retires — he may feel his whole life is over. Each person has an "internal director of affairs" that says what is right and good in terms of the jobs, feelings and functions regardless of society's sex-role stereotypes.[2] Some people like to work in the garden, others enjoy vacuuming or entertaining small children. We say people have a right to choose their functions in the family insofar as that is practical. In a family where nobody likes to wash dishes, then dishwashing has to be negotiated.

Openness to the Outside

Accessibility of the family to new ideas, places, people, things.

Is it possible for members to get out of, and back into, their family as their needs dictate? Are members relatively adventurous or do they always need the security of their home with its set routines and ideas? How do members feel about outsiders — comfortable or threatened? A family system that is open to outside influences is also receptive to the notion of change and flexibility. Families whose energy goes into protecting themselves from the outside have little energy left over to deal with the positive aspects of change.

[2] Eleanor Hamilton, from workshop, Cape Breton Island, Nova Scotia: "Sex Counseling, Process and Techniques," sponsored by Hamilton School Counseling Center, Sheffield, Mass., 1974.

Chapter 3
Negative Mechanisms

Mechanisms are individual, repeated behaviors that help the family function, or dysfunction. We are dealing in this book with Negative Mechanisms, that is, Mechanisms which contribute to poor family process. More examples of the Negative Mechanisms described below will be given in the sections on each exercise used in the interviews.

Errors

Mistakes in following our directions.

Unnecessary Questions and Complaints About the Exercises

Requests for extra explanation about our directions; also, deprecating remarks about our directions.

"I don't understand anything you mean." "Do you mean draw a house *together?*" "Can we use the crayons?" "How long do we have?" "I think you should explain better." "This exercise is pretty dumb." These questions and remarks are diversions and communication blockers, rather than expanders.

"It's Impossible" / "I Won't Play"

Successfully stopping the whole family's completing an exercise by bugging out ("I won't play") or by declaring "It's impossible."

A good example is a father's hoarding the crayons during the House Drawing exercise in the first interview so that no one else could use them and then declaring, "It's impossible for us all to draw a house together."

General Complaining

Expressions of discontent about the family.

"I never get a chance to speak," "There's never enough to eat around here," "Of course *I* always have to pick up the mess" — these are a few examples of general complaining.

Evasions

Circumlocutions or silence to avoid direct response to fact or feeling.

Statement: "I feel angry when you're late for dinner." Response: "It was raining tonight."

Denials

Refusing to admit the truth of a fact or feeling.

"I never said that." "Death doesn't bother me — I'm looking forward to it." "Business is bad, but that won't affect our family income."

Double Messages

Verbal and/or nonverbal communications that convey opposite meanings at once.

A nonverbal example of a double message would be someone beckoning to you with one hand while pushing you away with the other. A mixture of verbal and nonverbal would be someone saying to you, "I want to be close to you," while keeping you at a distance with a straight arm, turned back, fierce frown; or its reverse, a verbal "I don't need you," delivered with begging or beckoning gestures.[1] A purely verbal double message would be, "You know of course that we want your friends to feel at home here even though they do make so much noise. . . ." Most double messages are far subtler than these examples — the nonverbals will be less blatant; perhaps a tiny shrug, a slight, passing change of facial expression. The contradictory or opposite part of the verbal double message may rest only in the tone of voice. In all cases a double message does not jibe. Its effect is to confuse others. It is impossible for the listener to tell what the speaker means, for the speaker gives two opposing messages because he/she cannot decide which is the real one.

Answering for Others

Responding to a question asked of someone else.

Speaking for Others

Talking on behalf of another present person.

Giving Orders

Telling others what to do.

Placating

Keeping negative feelings from being expressed by appeasing behavior.

"A big help in doing a good placating job is to think of yourself as really worth nothing. . . as being physically down on one knee

---

[1]Virginia Satir, *Peoplemaking* (Palo Alto, Calif.: Science and Behavior Books, 1972), pp. 60, 61.

... putting out one hand in a begging fashion."[2] A true placater works overtime to keep everybody really happy — breaks up arguments and fights between others by offering platitudes, solutions, new teddy bears to the combatants; deflects any display of others' anger or pain by making sure their wants are met, sometimes even before they are expressed; and never, never expresses negative feelings. Having a placater in the family is like having a retinue of king's servants in constant attendance.

Blaming

Directly finding fault in others.

Sarcastic Remarks

Jibes or jeers – generally ironical.

Inappropriate Jokes

Humor used to avoid confronting facts or feelings.

"We laugh that we would not cry." While humor can be comforting and therapeutic, very often individuals or entire families use it to cover up feelings of anger, sadness, loneliness, or fear, laughing and joking away these feelings and any facts or circumstances that may trigger them. Such humor is inappropriate in that it blocks expression of negative feelings so they cannot be dealt with and resolved. One of our families was extraordinarily witty in talking about its disastrous financial plight. When we listened to the tape, much of the laughter sounded like sobbing.

Distractions

Diverting others' attention from current activity or feeling.[3]

[2] Ibid., p. 64.
[3] Ibid., p. 63.

Interruptions

Breaking into others' conversation or activity.

Defensive Long-Talking

Lengthy conversation to avoid confronting facts or feelings.

Like inappropriate joking, defensive long-talking covers and shoves away difficult feelings and the facts that trigger them.[4] But unlike joking it gives an outlet only to the talker, who may feel better after giving a long lecture on the ontological status of norms or whatever. Others, if they are still in the room when the talker has finished, are probably bored, angry, or confused — in no mood to relate in a positive way to the talker.

Putdowns

Deliberate attempts to lower the self-esteem of others.

Self-Putdowns

Statements of low assessment of one's own worth.

Bribes

Promises by one member to others of rewards for "voting" on his/her side during negotiations.

Threats

Statements of intention to hurt another person physically or emotionally if that person does not obey commands.

[4]Ibid., p. 63. Satir uses the term "human computer."

Defiance and Rule Breaking

Members' actions or statements clearly in opposition to each other, us, or our directions.

"Go ahead and ask me questions, but I won't answer them," snarled a teenager at us from the depths of a wing chair while his brother breathed vapor onto our microphone so that it wouldn't pick up sound for the next few minutes. These were mild examples, directed at us, of defiance and rule breaking we saw go on almost continuously in this family.

Fake Placating

Insincere appeasing or agreeableness.

"Why, Sweetie Pie, of course I agree with you," says the wife in dulcet tones in the midst of a shouting match. "Anything you say, Dear." Fake placating will make chills run up and down your spine.

Each family has it ways of provoking one another, defending against feelings, and letting feelings out sideways. As you notice other Negative Mechanisms, you can list them. Some others we found were *lies, loud screaming, warning, whining, foul language, interpreting for others.*

Chapter 4
Family Dynamics

Family Dynamics are forces operating in the family system: repeated larger behavior patterns, conscious or subconscious, in which two or more members consistently interrelate; and the powerful, prevailing attitudes or emotional climates that contribute to the family's process. We are mostly dealing here with dysfunctional Dynamics; functional Dynamics are included in Skills. However, the Dynamics of *boundaries; sharing about sex, money, death,* and *"misfortune"*; and the emotional climates of *anger, fear,* and *warmth and emotional support* are common to all families and can be seen positively as well as negatively.

Collusions

Unspoken agreements, between two or more family members, which negate family growth.

Collusion, in the strict sense, would apply to all the Family Dynamics listed below and indeed to most Negative Mechanisms. The interactions we are calling collusions are those that do not have a ready name, unlike scapegoating, hidden agendas, assumption making, and others. An example: Jack Brown has never been able to hold a job for more than six months.[1] He is too clumsy to help around the house. He cannot

---

[1] To illustrate some Negative Family Dynamics we are using a hypothetical family, the Browns: Jack, Lucy, Nate, Sara, and Danny.

help get the children off to school because he is too disorganized. We also see, however, that he is charming and agreeable all the time — is never angry at the children and is extremely sympathetic to his wife, Lucy, when she feels overwhelmed by her full-time, low-paying job and all the household duties. The Brown family wants to keep Jack charming, agreeable, and sympathetic. Lucy wants to be a martyr. Their method of maintaining their process is to collude with him in the fiction that he is helpless, clumsy, and irresponsible. The collusion negates family growth. How can the Browns learn to negotiate if one member's behavior is nonnegotiable? How can the children learn about responsibility and internally chosen roles if the parents model a system in which one person does nothing and the other does all? How can Jack or Lucy make personal changes, even if they have the desire, if the whole system is set up to keep them both exactly the way they are?

Secrets, Myths, Taboos

Deliberately unshared information, deliberately kept family fiction. Forbidden subjects.

In the Brown family all these play into the family collusion. The myth is that Jack is the head of the household, roost-ruler — everyone must treat him that way; his nickname is "Boss." It is taboo in the family to mention his job losses or even the family's iffy financial state. The secret, kept by both parents from the children, is that Jack was an illegitimate baby whose alcoholic father left his mother before he was born, never to be heard from again.

Hidden Agenda

An individual's unspoken needs, wishes, or emotional conflicts.

Lucy Brown, whose father left when she was five, has a desperate fear of being abandoned that she does not admit. Her hidden agenda, the unspoken need, as she takes on more and more responsibility, is, "Don't leave me, Jack." She cannot express the anger she feels about her position either; by her reasoning, that will be sure to drive Jack away from her. She is caught in a bind of never being able to state her real feelings.

Assumption Making

Believing you know the facts, feelings, and/or motivations involving other members without checking them out.

Jack Brown assumes his wife likes doing all the housework. He has never checked out, as he sees her doing all the laundry, whether or not she enjoys doing it. And she has never directly told him how much she resents it — she is afraid her anger will drive him away. Also, she assumes that he enjoys sitting around the house all day doing nothing.

Scapegoating

The singling out of one member as the cause of family problems and the recipient of family anger.[2]

In the Brown family the younger boy, Danny, is dyslexic, messy, sassy, and a troublemaker. Lucy, with everyone else colluding, has singled him out to dump her anger on, standing him in for her father and her husband to whom she can't show anger. "If it weren't for you, everyone would be happy in this family," she often sighs. He responds by acting out the whole family's pain in his disruptive behavior.

[2]Kenneth J. Olson, "An Investigation of Scapegoating, Favoritism, and Self-Blame in Families," *Dissertation Abstracts,* vol. 29 [2-A] (1968), pp. 484–485; Norman Paul and Joseph D. Bloom, "Multiple Family Therapy: Secrets and Scapegoating in Family Crisis," *International Journal of Psychotherapy,* vol. 20, no. 1 (1970), pp. 37–47.

Power

The uneven, inappropriate use of, or struggle for, authority or influence by some members to control the lives of others.

In the Brown family, the members have no positive power. They are all locked into an unchanging system. Each person uses what power he/she has to maintain an unhealthy process: Jack, his helplessness; Lucy, her willingness to be a martyr; Sara, siding with mother; Nate, good-boy attention getter; Danny, troublemaker. Other families may have hierarchical power systems in which one person sets rules, gives orders, makes decisions. In a healthy system all members have equal rights, appropriate to their ages and needs, giving the whole family power to change.

Boundaries

Members' limits for individual privacy, protection, self-definition. Also family definition to the outside world.

Lucy Brown has no personal boundaries — she is constantly invaded by the needs of others, she cannot say no, nor can she find time or space to develop her own interests. The family boundaries, however, are closed. The family does not share its plight with anyone outside nor can the older boy leave home to get a summer job — "I need you at home," says Mrs. Brown. In a healthy family, all members would have the right to space and time for themselves, and the ability to state their boundaries. The family would feel easy about its family boundaries, allowing its members to come and go and to bring in information in the form of friends and new and different ideas and styles.

Family Alliances

Subgroups banding together for protection and/or power.

In the Brown family the mother and daughter are very close — in alliance against the males. Family alliances are not always sex-linked — they may be any combination of members, and there may be several subgroup alliances in one family. These alliances may shift according to who's home at any given time. When Grandmother comes to stay, there may be a realignment according to whom she needs on her side. In healthy families there is free flow among members, and no rigid alliances form.

Sexism

Limitations and expectations of an individual based on his/her being male/female.

In the Brown family it is expected that Lucy Brown will do the housework and that her daughter, Sara, will help her. The older son, Nate, will mow the lawn. He would like to take over the cooking because he is fascinated by food, but his mother and sister tell him to get out of the kitchen. Since Nate is a "good" boy, he obediently mows the lawn. This family is set up to teach the children that men are to be served by women, that men and women are different, the sex barrier can never be crossed.

Sharing About Sex, Money, Death, "Misfortune"

Family ability to be open with each other in dealing with all of these subjects.

The Brown family has many real problems, but they cannot face them or share their feelings about them with each other. They use many Negative Mechanisms — evasions, denials, placating, direct lying to avoid dealing with facts or emotions around all these subjects.

Each time there is a financial crisis, the parents focus their feelings on the problems of Danny — it is the need for special tutoring which causes the overdraft at the bank rather than Jack's inability to keep a job or Lucy's unwillingness to take herself seriously enough to get a good job.

The children's information on sex has come only from friends at school. They cannot ask either parent about menstruation, nocturnal emissions, masturbation, birth control, pregnancy, venereal diseases, abortion, or miscarriage. Nor can they discuss with them any of their homosexual or heterosexual experiences, fearing that they may be abnormal or that their parents will not approve. Jack and Lucy are embarrassed to talk about their own sexuality with each other.

Death has never been mentioned except in undertones last year when Grandmother was very ill. Jack and Lucy feel too frightened themselves to be able to share any facts or feelings about it with the children.

In a healthy family, all of the members share in talking about these subjects with each other. Appropriate facts are openly discussed; the feelings of each person are heard and respected.

Anger

"Emotional agitation aroused by great displeasure"[3] *directly or indirectly expressed and heard.*

To further quote *Webster's New World Dictionary,* anger is "a feeling that may result from injury, mistreatment, opposition etc.: it usually shows itself in a desire to hit out at something or someone else...." We would add that a healthy family would have an emotional climate in which feelings of anger would be allowed to be expressed verbally whenever and to whomever appropriate. Anger treated in this way in the family does not become repressed and take on the many forms of stylized repeated responses we are all familiar with — sulking, nagging, chronic forgetfulness, heavy drinking, physical brutality. Everyone needs to express anger directly some of the time. In the Brown family, no one can express anger at Jack, the children cannot directly express anger at either parent. Jack cannot express anger directly at anyone (he is so charming and easygoing).

[3]*Webster's New World Dictionary,* college edition (New York: World Publishing Co., 1964).

Fear

"Feeling of anxiety and agitation caused by the presence or nearness of danger"[4] *openly or directly expressed and heard, or hidden and expressed indirectly.*

As with anger, in the emotional climate of a healthy family feelings of fear would be openly expressed and heard. Fear treated respectfully does not become repressed and displaced, to come out in unhealthy ways such as hypochondria, nightmares, phobias, and paranoia. If children are laughed at or told "don't be afraid of that," they will learn quickly that being afraid is not acceptable. The fear will not go away; it will go underground. Grownups, too, are often afraid and need to share their fears without threat of ridicule. It is helpful for children to know that their parents sometimes have fears, can share and help each other to overcome those fears. The Brown family is fearful of many things in the outside world. No specific fears are talked about, but when Nate wants to go away to a summer job, Lucy says, "I need you at home." Nate has the idea that the outside world is dangerous, and although he is willing to give it a try, his mother's fear keeps him at home.

Warmth and Emotional Support

Direct caring between members based on mutual commitment to the growth of others.

In the Brown family, some of the warmth and caring is based on fear and need. Lucy and Sara care about each other, but they need each other as allies and cannot have a very honest relationship for fear of losing each other in the hostile world of males they both feel they live in. The males are not very warm and caring about each other, nor do they give each other much emotional support. In their view, males are not supposed to need

[4]Ibid.

such support. Jack gets it sometimes alone with Lucy, but the boys never get it.

In a healthy family members have free access to one another, physically and emotionally meet each others' needs for closeness, and support each others' needs to be individuals. Boy children and girl children are treated with the same amounts and kinds of caring by both parents. And the parents model together genuine and open displays of love and affection.

Chapter 5
The Interview Kit

The Interview Kit contains all the forms you will need for the three interviews with a family. All the forms here are blank and may be duplicated for your own use. In Appendix 3 (pages 166–181) there is a duplicate set filled in with information about our sample Smith family. (After you have reviewed the blank forms, notice how we filled in the forms for the Smith family.)

In each of the chapters that follow on the three interviews there are complete instructions on when and how to fill in the forms. We introduce the Interview Kit here so you will be familiar with the forms before we give all the instructions.

The Interview Kit includes the following:

- Interview I
- Interview II
- Interview III
- History Taking Form
- History Taking Analysis
- Skills Sheet
- Negative Mechanisms Sheet
- Family Dynamics/Nonverbal Sheet
- Summary Sheet

THE SKILLS SHEET

The "Skills Sheet" is a form for scoring families' Skills all on one page. The main section will be filled out after each of the first two interviews, using either the assessment suggestions with each exercise or the scoring directions in Appendix 2. We have provided columns for averages of each Skill, for average total Skill scores for each exercise, and for averages in the four Skill-grouped areas. When filled out after Interviews I and II, these columns will help you to see a score based on more than one exercise; what kind of exercises the family does well at; and how the family scores in each of the four areas. Starting at the bottom of the Skills Sheet and continuing on the back, we have given you room for *"Notes on Each Skill."* These will be brief descriptions of the family's Skills. They will be helpful when you make up the Summary Sheet for Feedback in Interview III.

NEGATIVE MECHANISMS SHEET

The "Negative Mechanisms Sheet" will help you keep track of the number of Negative Mechanisms a family uses during five exercises. You can fill it out as you listen to the tapes after each interview. Then fill in the two *"total"* columns at the side and on the bottom. The side totals will tell you how many of each Mechanism a family uses during all five exercises. The bottom totals will tell you how the family responds to each exercise. If, for example, they have a far higher number at the bottom of the Bonanza column than the Problem column, you will know the family has trouble with issues involved in Bonanza.

At the right of the page, you will see two summation boxes, handy during the Feedback in Interview III.

FAMILY DYNAMICS / NONVERBAL SHEET

The "Family Dynamics Sheet" has two parts: the front for notes on Family Dynamics for each exercise; the back for notes on nonverbal observations for each exercise. These are not scored in the way Skills or Negative Mechanisms are. When you have finished an exercise and are evaluating it, write notes on the sheet of any of the Family Dynamics we list, or any others you might discover. These notes will help you see the broader pattern of a family, particularly as you see the Dynamics repeated in several games.

Nonverbal Notes

Many books have been written about the nonverbal behavior of human beings.[1] Make note of the patterns of interacting and patterns of individual behavior. What a smile means in your family may not mean the same in another. Your mother may have been pleased and proud of you. Your friend's mother may be smiling because she is embarrassed when one of her children speaks. In *Kinesics and Context,* Ray Birdwhistell says:

> Insofar as I have been able to determine, just as there are no universal words, no sound complexes, which carry the same meaning the world over, there are no body motions, facial expressions, or gestures which provoke identical responses the world over. A body can be bowed in grief, in humility, in laughter, or in readiness for aggression. A "smile" in one society portrays friendliness, in another embarrassment, and, in still another, may contain a warning that unless tension is reduced, hostility and attack will follow.[2]

Observe the individuals in the family as closely as possible during each exercise for the kinds of nonverbal defenses each uses. Do they barricade themselves behind furniture; leave the room when feelings run high; smoke, eat, or drink continually; do things compulsively like pipe-tapping, dog-patting, ashtray-emptying? Do they touch their own bodies — face rubbing, fingernail biting, hair twirling? Is their appearance extraordinarily dirty, messy, or extraordinarily clean, neat? Do they hold

---

[1] Gregory Bateson and Margaret Mead, *Balinese Character: A Photographic Analysis* (New York: Special Publications of the New York Academy of Sciences, vol. 2, 1942); Seymour Fisher, *Body Consciousness* (Englewood Cliffs, N.J.: Prentice-Hall, 1973); Arnold Gesell, *The Child from Five to Ten* (New York: Harper, 1946); William J. Lederer and Don D. Jackson, *The Mirages of Marriage* (New York: Norton, 1968).

[2] Ray Birdwhistell, *Kinesics and Context* (Philadelphia: University of Pennsylvania Press, 1970).

a lot of tension in their bodies or face — worry wrinkles, permanently down-turned mouth? How do they relate spatially to each other — can they get close or do they always sit a yard apart from one another? Does anyone place h/self continually outside the family group? Are they relaxed or are they nervous, spacy, or vague? Do you notice a patterned sequence of events? For example, in one family, whenever the mother and father began to argue, the two daughters moved physically between them. The oldest daughter always moved next to the mother and the youngest next to the father.

THE SUMMARY SHEET

The "Summary Sheet" is designed as a one-page summation to help you during the Feedback in Interview III. It sometimes happened that there were long gaps between interviews because of illness, vacations or other reasons, or we saw more than one family concurrently and would forget by the last interview what all our scribbling had meant. It seemed logical to get it all onto one piece of paper for the final interview, for purposes of review for ourselves, and so as not to be shuffling around several pieces of paper during the Feedback.

If you will look at the Summary Sheet, pp. 58–59, you will see that it has places for notes on:

"Inherited Family Process": A précis of the most important things you have written in the History Taking Analysis.

"Present Family Process": A brief analysis of the family's communication and problem-solving abilities, self-esteem, receptivity to growth and change; notes on all relevant Negative Mechanisms; and notes on Family Dynamics.

" 'Contract' Between Husband and Wife": Brief description, as you see it.

"Sculpture Comments": Filled out after the last interview since the Sculpture is done during Interview III. It is a convenient place for you to have a few notes for later reference.

"Stated Present Problems": A brief statement of the family's problems as the family sees them.

"Problems as I See Them": The family's view of their problems may not be the same as yours, in that they will often see the problem as being

invested all in one person, a troubled teenager, a depressed mother, an alcoholic father. You may see the problem quite differently. For example, as a lack of ability in the Skills involved in communication. It is important to write down what you think since you will be making a contract with them (or referring them elsewhere), and it would be colluding in their process to agree with their myth that the problem is little Johnny. This is not to disallow that little Johnny is a problem.

"Family's Goals": A summary of what the family say they want to achieve in their work in therapy. This will remind you when making a contract to pay attention to what they say, and to whether you feel you can work with them toward those goals.

"Contract Needed with Family": Once you have done the evaluating necessary to go into the third interview, you will have to decide, if you are going to work with any family, how you are going to see them. In the section on contract making, page 113, we will talk more about this, but here is a place to write down what kind of a contract you want to make so you will not be put off by the hesitancy or hostility of some members of the family.

INTERVIEW I (2 hours)

History Taking (90 minutes)

Equipment

Tape recorder
All five pages of History Taking forms with one copy of page 5 for each child in the family

Directions to the Family

I am going to ask you a lot of questions to help us all find out more about your family. I'd like each of you to respond to the first few questions. Then I'm going to ask [*husband and wife – call them by their names*] about their grandparents and parents and what it was like for them growing up, and when they were first married. Finally I'm going to ask each child starting with the oldest [*call him/her by name*] some questions about yourselves and what you think it's like to live in your family. This will take about an hour and a half all told. I would like all of you to feel free to speak up if you hear any answers that are surprises to you, or new to you, or that you don't understand.

Draw a House (30 minutes)

Equipment

Tape recorder
A large piece of paper and a box of crayons

Directions to the Family

This is a nonverbal exercise — that means no talking to each other or to me. I'd like you to use these crayons and this paper to draw a house together for your family. You have ten minutes. *(Ask them each to put themselves in the drawing if they don't do so spontaneously.)*

Ask each member: What house were you drawing?

Ask the whole family: Were there surprises or were all of you aware what house you were drawing together?

INTERVIEW II (1 hour 50 minutes)

Role Card Game (30 minutes)

Equipment

Tape recorder
36 Role Cards (see list p. 75)
A piece of paper, pencil, and elastic for each member

Directions to the Family

I'm going to lay out a bunch of cards. I'd like each of you to pick up the cards that are accurate for you and lay them in front of you on the table so that others can see them. If someone picks up a card you feel belongs to you, write it on the paper in front of you. Please wait till everybody has a chance to see all the cards before you pick them up. This is going to be a nonverbal game — that means no talking. If you don't know the meaning of a card, please ask me, not each other.

Now I'd like you, one at a time, first to check out whether your cards are all accurate for you. Next, check out each other person's cards. Say, into the tape recorder, if you think a card they have is not accurate for them. Also say into the tape recorder if you think a card you or someone else has picked, or a card that is left over, belongs to them.

If someone gives you a card that you think is wrong for you, say, into the tape recorder, "I think 'Disciplinarian' is wrong for me." Then put the card into a separate "Wrong" pile or write it on your paper as "Wrong" if someone else already has possession of the card.

Now is your chance to get rid of any roles you do not like, even though they may be correct for you. Discard the role onto the center of the table. Go one at a time, and say what you are doing into the tape recorder.

Ask each member: Do you have any fun together at dinner and in the evening?

Family Problems (20 minutes)

Equipment

Tape recorder
Pencil and cards for each member

Directions to the Family

Every family has problems, some bigger than others. I'd like each of you to write down on your cards what you think is the biggest problem in your family. Then hand the cards to me. I won't show them to anyone else in the family. Please don't talk to each other while you're writing.

Now I'd like you all to discuss the problems in your family for ten or fifteen minutes. Each person try to respond to each problem.

Asking for What You Want (30 minutes)

Equipment

Tape recorder
A pencil and two cards for each member — a Want Card and a Question Card

Directions to the Family

I'd like each of you to write down on these Want Cards what you want most from each person in the family. Next, write down what you think each person wants from you. Please don't talk to each other.

Now I'd like each of you to ask each person in the family directly for what you want most from them for yourself. Everybody please try to respond. You can be brief — this should take about one minute per transaction.

Each of you please fill out these Question Cards: What did each person ask you for? Do you think you can give it to them? Do you think you can get what you asked for from them?

Family Bonanza (30 minutes)

Equipment

Tape recorder
A "check" for the yearly family income
Pencils and cards for each member

Directions to the Family

I'm giving your family a check. I'd like each of you to think privately, without talking, about how you would like your family to spend the money, and write it on the cards. You may keep your cards during this exercise. Then, each of you say how you'd like to spend the money. Then I'd like the whole family to negotiate together how you would all spend the money. Each of you try to get what you want. You have about ten minutes.

Write down on the back of the "check" how you will spend the money. Put next to each item how much money you'll spend on it.

Each of you please initial the list if you agree with it.

INTERVIEW III (timing up to you)

Family Sculpture

Explain to the family briefly what Family Sculpture is.

Starting with the parents, ask them to show, in sculptural terms, what their relationship was like at the point they decided to get married.

Ask each child, starting with the oldest, to add h/self sculpturally to the family. Help the family adjust its special relationships as each additional member gets "born."

When all members are in the sculpture, ask the family if their relationships to each other feel accurate — is that how it is in the family now? Allow them time, if necessary, to sculpt themselves as they are in the present.

Feedback

Discussion with the family on the following

1. Family Process
    Strengths
    Weaknesses

2. Skills
    Communication: Straight Talking/Responding; Listening; Shared Facts, Meanings, Values
    Problem Solving: Risk Taking; Openness Intra Family; Negotiating; Decision Making; Responsibility
    Family Self-Esteem: Positive Contact with Each Other; Ability to Play; Ability to Get What You Want
    Receptivity to Growth and Change: Accepting Individual Differences; Limit Setting; Internally Chosen Roles; Openness to the Outside
3. Factors Negating Family Growth
    Negative Mechanisms
    Dysfunctional Family Dynamics
4. Factors Promoting Family Growth
    Lack of Negative Mechanisms
    Functional Family Dynamics
5. Sculpture Comments
6. Family Comments on You
7. Contract or Referral

When a Family Needs Therapy

History Taking (page 1)   Name:_____

I. Ask Each Family Member: (10 minutes total)

Each of you please share with me why you are here.
Is anyone important not here?
What is your occupation?
What is your yearly family income?
What is your religion?

II. Ask Husband and Wife about Their Grandparents: (5 minutes total)

	Husband Paternal Grandparents		Wife Paternal Grandparents	
	Grandfather	Grandmother	Grandfather	Grandmother
where born				
when die				
what kind of person was he/she				

	Maternal Grandparents		Maternal Grandparents	
	Grandfather	Grandmother	Grandfather	Grandmother
where born				
when die				
what kind of person was he/she				

History Taking (page 2)   Name: _____

III. Ask Husband and Wife about Their Parents: (15 minutes total)

| | Husband || Wife ||
	Father	Mother	Father	Mother
still alive (when die)				
marriage date				
divorces # marriages				
occupation unemployment				
abortions miscarriages				
religion				
how did they get along				
how did they show caring				
what was their sex life like				
how did they show anger				
physical violence				
alcohol				
physical illness				
emotional problems - seek help				
who made decisions				
who made rules				
who handled money				

History Taking (page 3)   Name:_____

IV. Ask Husband and Wife about Their Upbringing: (20 minutes total)

	Husband	Wife
date of birth		
planned/ unplanned		
sibs birth order		
how did you get along with parents		
how did you get what you wanted		
how were you punished		
how did you show anger		
how did you show physical affection		
what do you think your family expected of you		
emotional problems		
illness accidents		
problems of sibs		
what was most significant death		
how was that death handled		
how did you feel about yourself growing up		
how do you feel about yourself now		

History Taking (page 4)   Name:_____

V. Ask Husband and Wife about Their Life Together: (20 minutes total)

	Husband	Wife
date of marriage/ former marriages		
what attracted you to him/her		
what made you decide to marry		
did "honeymoon" live up to expectations		
what was your sex life like then		
what is your sex life like now		
did you discuss having kids		
were children planned/unplanned ask re each child		
miscarriages		
abortions		
did your relationship change once you had kids		
friends - social life		
how do you show anger to each other		
how do you show caring to each other		
what are the rules in the family now		
taboo subjects in family		
problems with alcohol		
have you ever considered separation or divorce		

History Taking (page 5)   Name:_____

VI. Ask Each Child about His/Her Life: (10 minutes each)

date of birth	
how do you get along with sibs	
illness accidents	
how are you doing in school	
friends	
sex education	
drugs/alcohol	
moving	
what are the rules in this family	
how are you punished/ who punishes you	
how do you think your parents get along-- show caring to each other show anger to each other	
how do you show caring and to whom	
how do you show anger and to whom	
how do you get what you want in your family	
do you think there are taboo subjects in family	
do you think you have a special role in this family	
how do you feel about yourself	

51 The Interview Kit

History Taking Analysis   Name:_____

Husband: Name:_____   Date of Birth:_____
Family Background:

Personal History:

Wife: Name:_____   Date of Birth:_____
Family Background:

Personal History:

(over)

History Taking Analysis (page 2)

Child #1:   Name:_____   Date of Birth:_____

Personal History:

Child #2:   Name:_____   Date of Birth:_____

Personal History:

53 The Interview Kit

Skills Sheet

Name:_____

Family Members:_____

Skills	Exercises					Aver. for Skill	Skill-Grouped Score (Average)
	House	Roles	Prob	Askg	Bon		
Straight Talking/ Responding							Communication
Listening							
Shared Facts, Meanings, Values							
Risk Taking							Problem Solving
Openness intra Family							
Negotiating							
Decision Making							
Responsibility							
Positive Contact with Each Other							Family Self-Esteem
Ability to Play							
Ability to Get What You Want							
Accepting Individual Differences							Receptivity to Growth and Change
Limit Setting							
Internally Chosen Roles							
Openness to the Outside							
Average Score for Each Exercise:							

Notes on Each Skill:

When a Family Needs Therapy 54

Negative Mechanisms Sheet   Name: _____

Negative Mechanisms	Exercises						Major Factors Inhibiting Family Growth: (list highest totals)
	House	Roles	Prob	Askg	Bon	Total	
Errors							
Unnecessary Questions and Complaints re ex.							
"It's Impossible" "I Won't Play"							
General Complaining							
Evasions							
Denials							
Double Messages							
Answering for Others							
Speaking for Others							
Giving Orders							
Placating							
Blaming							
Sarcastic Remarks							
Inappropriate Jokes							Family is Largely Free of: (list lowest totals)
Distractions							
Interruptions							
Defensive Long-Talking							
Putdowns							
Self-Putdowns							
Lies							
Bribes							
Threats							
Defiance/Rulebreaking							
Loud Screaming							
Fake Placating							
Other:							
Total for Each Exercise:							

(over)

Negative Mechanisms Notes:

Family Dynamics Sheet   Name:_____

History Taking:

Draw a House:

Role Card Game:

Family Problems:

Asking for What you Want:

Family Bonanza:

Family Sculpture:

(over)

57 The Interview Kit

Nonverbal Notes on Exercises

History Taking:

Draw a House:

Role Card Game:

Family Problems:

Asking for What You Want

Family Bonanza:

Family Sculpture:

Summary Sheet

Inherited Family Process:

Present Family Process:

"Contract" between Husband and Wife:

(over)

59 The Interview Kit

Summary Sheet (page 2)

Sculpture Comments:

Stated Present Problems:

Problems as I See Them:

Family's Goals:

Contract Needed with Family:

Chapter 6

Interview 1

HISTORY TAKING
DRAW A HOUSE

HISTORY TAKING (90 minutes)

Description of Exercise

Ask the members about their family history, from husband's and wife's grandparents to the present, using the sequential questions on the five-page History Taking form in the Interview Kit (pages 46–50).

    The purpose of taking a fairly full history from each member of the family is to help you find out about the family's process: which ways of dealing with events get handed down through the generations? How does the family deal with events now? In the course of the History Takings we did, some of our families made connections for themselves about their process — that the youngest child always becomes a message carrier for instance, that no one in the family is ever allowed to express angry feelings, that women are not supposed to act educated. None of our families had ever sat down all together and talked about themselves and their histories in such a concentrated way. One family found the History Taking to be the most revealing of all of the exercises, and said it freed them to talk together and understand each other more.

Equipment

Tape recorder
History Taking form with one copy of page 5 for each child in the family

Directions to the Family

Tell the family you are going to take a detailed history from each of them in order that they, and you, can learn about how their family got to be the way it is. Tell them how long it will take, and ask them to please be patient. Say, particularly to the children: "If you hear any answers that are a surprise to you or new to you, or that you don't understand, please speak up."

Directions for Interviewer

Ask each family member to respond to the questions in section I of the History Taking form. Then let husband and wife decide who wants to be questioned first on their history. Maintain continuity by asking all the questions — sections II, III, IV — of spouse 1, then ask the same questions of spouse 2. Finally ask them both to respond to the questions in section V about each other. Question the children in order of their age, if possible; oldest first. Try to keep the momentum of the History Taking going without actually rushing the family; otherwise it can go on for hours. We took almost five hours to do one family of four people. Their history was complex. All the members had difficulty answering the questions directly, so that we had to ask each question several times, and we allowed ourselves to become sidetracked on issues that interested us rather than sticking only to the questions at hand. We all ended up exhausted, and found that the extra hours we'd spent were not particularly helpful in terms of extra information.

Children. With small children, you may have to ask their questions first in order to allow them to play, or whatever. You will have to rephrase some of their questions so they can understand them — for instance, "How do you show anger?" could be rephrased, "When you're really mad at your mom, what kinds of things do you do?" If the child needs more help, then ask, "Do you yell?" "Do you mess up your room?" etc. If the child still can't answer, you can encourage him/her by saying something like, "You know, everybody gets angry sometimes — when I was little, I used to hide under my bed. . . ." Be aware that children under about five may have a hard time answering any of the questions. If so, ask them their birthday, and whatever else they can answer, and then ask the rest of the family to answer the other questions for them. It is better not to push children who can't answer the history questions than to risk turning them off so they can't cooperate in the exercises that follow.

ASSESSING THE HISTORY TAKING

Write down your assessment comments on the sheets provided in the Kit. (*Note:* No numerical scoring is necessary on the Skills sheet and Negative Mechanisms sheet for this exercise.)

If you wish to use our scoring system for this exercise, see Appendix 2.

Skills

1. *Straight Talking/Responding.* Throughout the History Taking notice whether the members answer your questions directly. If they space off, evade, act confused or nervous, note if you think you have hit on a family secret or taboo, e.g., a grandfather nobody is allowed to discuss because . . . Why? Mother and Father's wedding date is unknown because . . . a child born "too early"?

2. *Shared Facts, Meanings, Values.* Be aware throughout whether there are agreements or discrepancies among family members about the facts. If there are significant discrepancies, you can use them as clues to look for family secrets or taboos.

Questions that check for shared meanings and values are all in section I of the History Taking, addressed to all family members.
"Each of you please share with me why you are here."
"Is anyone important not here?"
"What is your religion?"

3. *Openness Intra Family.*
   (to parents)
   "How did your parents get along?"
   "Were you planned/unplanned?"
   "How did you get along with your parents?"
   "What made you decide to marry?"
   "Did your honeymoon live up to expectations?"
   "Did you discuss having kids?"
   "Were your children planned/unplanned?"
   "Have you ever considered separation or divorce?"
   (to kids)
   "Do you get along with your brothers and sisters?"

In an open family there should be some leeway for stating negative answers to these questions as well as positive ones ("everybody always got along just fine — no, no fights"). An open family will have discussed feelings about having children before conceiving them, will have talked with their children about their births, and will have made a decision to live together or marry, weighing the cons as well as the pros. ("We never need to talk about those things — we all think alike" is a nonanswer.)

4. *Responsibility.* Do both parents, and children, where appropriate, share breadwinning roles:
   "What is your occupation?"
   "What is your yearly income?"

5. *Positive Contact with Each Other.*
   (to parents)
   "How did your parents show caring?"
   "How did you show physical affection when you were a child?"

"How do you show caring to each other now?"
(to kids)
"How do you think your parents show caring to each other?"
"How do you show caring, and to whom?"

In families where there is free positive access to one another, these questions will be answered easily, with eye contact and smiles between the members. Other families will have trouble with the questions, evading direct answers, acting giggly, or nervous, or even demonstrating mock affection. In one family we interviewed the husband demonstrated how his parents showed caring by woodenly embracing his wife, who stiffened as he kissed her on the lips.

6. *Ability to Get What You Want.*
(to parents)
"How did you get what you wanted when growing up?"
"How did you feel about yourself when growing up?"
"How do you feel about yourself now?"
(to kids)
"How do you get what you want?"
"How do you feel about yourself?"

Look for direct answers that indicate the confidence to ask specific people for specific emotional support, and that show good feelings about self. Qualified answers, "I don't know's," and vague rambling can indicate an inability to get, as can direct negative answers — "I never get anything I want around here and I feel awful about myself."

7. *Limit Setting.*
(to parents)
"How were you punished as a child?"
"What are the rules in the family now?"
(to kids)
"What are the rules in this family?"
"How are you punished/who punishes you?"

Who disciplines or punishes, and who gets disciplined or punished? Not the kind of punishment — beating, deprivation, isolation treatment. Some families have few apparent rules, no punishment, and yet the children are very docile. Look for underground messages about misbehavior, like a parent who gets heart trouble whenever a child acts "bad." Other families have many rules, many punishments, and yet the kids are in constant "trouble" — at school, at home, even with the police. Acting "bad" in these families may be a way of getting attention from parents.

   8. *Internally Chosen Roles.*
      (to parents — in reference to their parents)
      "Who made the decisions?"
      "Who made the rules?"
      "Who handled the money?"
Answers will tell you whether the families of origin openly shared power roles — decision making and handling money — or whether they operated along traditional sex lines: "Oh, Father definitely ruled the roost." "Mother did everything — but always deferred to Father whenever he voiced an opinion [or] always made it look like Father was the boss." "Father always said Mother was too dumb to handle money" or "Father made the money, Mother spent it." "Father was never home — Mother handled everything in the house."
      (to parents)
      "What do you think your family expected of you?"
      (to kids)
      "Do you think you have a special role in this family?"
Answers here will tell you whether children are encouraged to choose freely how they will function in the family, or whether their roles are predecided for them by their parents. If the parents had heavy expectations laid on them by their parents, take very careful note of how the children answer the questions about their special roles — chances are there will be the same kind of expectations: "be smart"; "help around the house". . . . Perhaps only one child will have to take on these roles and others will be allowed to choose more freely. It is important to note birth order here. Roles and expectations very often travel generationally

from oldest children to oldest children (or youngest to youngest, or middle to middle). That is, an "oldest" parent will decide that an oldest child is going to be exactly like him/her, and will impose on the child the same parental expectations imposed on him/her.

   9. *Openness to the Outside.*
     (to parents)
     "Do you have friends — what is your social life like?"
     (to kids)
     "How are you doing in school?"
     "Do you have friends?"

Are members open to people, places, and ideas? Do friends come easily in and out of the house? Are kids able to function in school — away from the familiarity of home?

Negative Mechanisms

Although all of the family's Negative Mechanisms will probably appear in a ninety-minute History Taking, we did not chart them in the histories we took as we found them to be pretty much a duplicate of the Mechanisms that appear in the exercises that follow, which we scored quite intricately. The only reason it would be useful for you to go over the tape carefully for all putdowns, evasions, denials and other Negative Mechanisms would be if you are using only the History Taking to interview the family, and are omitting the other exercises.

Family Dynamics

   1. *Secrets, Myths, Taboos.*
     (to parents and kids)
     "Do you think there are taboo subjects in this family?"

Most taboos in the families we interviewed had to do with sex, money, or emotional illness — there was a heavy ban on talking about these subjects. There were of course some highly individual and specific secrets, myths, and taboos in our families — a "strangely swarthy" great-grandmother (a gypsy?) whose name nobody knew; references to a grandfather who "may have killed his first wife." A family intent on maintaining its secrets, myths, and taboos will answer glibly that there are no taboo subjects in the family, although a child will often spill the beans by saying "You just can't talk about *anything* in this family!"

2. *Anger.*
    (to parents)
    "How did your parents show anger?"
    "Was there any physical violence?"
    "How did you show anger growing up?"
    "How do you show anger to each other now?"
    (to kids)
    "How do your parents show anger to each other?"
    "How do you show anger and to whom?"

Watch for process here. What methods of showing or muffling anger are passed down generationally? Does anger ever explode into physical violence? Are there injunctions never to show anger? Is it permissible to be angry at some people and not others? Does only one person exhibit all the family anger?

3. *Sex.*
    (to parents)
    "What was your parents' sex life like?"
    "What was your sex life like when you were first married?"
    "What is your sex life like now?"
    (to kids)
    "What has been your sex education?"

Note how members talk about sex as well as what they say. Are they giggly, shocked, or relaxed? Are children able to talk freely about sex with both their parents? In one of our families the parents refused to answer any of the questions about sex, and told us we should not ask such questions in front of children. We found a real taboo about sex in this family: their inability to talk about it and their anger at our questions lead us to believe that the parents do not relate openly together on a sexual level, and that they probably use sex as an anger release. We feel, moreover, that the children in the family have a strong injunction from the parents not to engage in sexual relationships in a healthy, exploring way.

  4. *Death.*
     (to parents)
     "What was the most significant death when growing up?"
     "How was that death handled?"

You will want to find out here if the feelings concerning the death were dealt with: was there a real mourning process, were people allowed to cry? Or was the family enjoined to keep a collective stiff upper lip and pretend nothing happened? An inability or a taboo about dealing with the feelings concerning death can breed sadness, depression, and anger that lie underground for years.

  5. *"Misfortune."*
     (to parents)
     "Did your mother have any abortions or miscarriages?"
     "Were there any problems with alcohol?"
     "Were there any physical illnesses in your family?"
     "Did anyone in your family have emotional problems? Did they seek help?"
     "Did you have any emotional problems growing up?"
     "Did you have any illnesses or accidents?"
     "Did your sisters/brothers have problems?"
     "Have you ever had a miscarriage?"
     "Have you ever had an abortion?"
     "Have you ever had problems with alcohol?"
     (to kids)
     "Have you had any illnesses or accidents?"
     "Have you had problems with drugs or alcohol?"
     "Have there been any significant moves?"

Look for process in the answers to these questions — is there a history of emotional illness or alcoholism in the family? Are people accident prone? Also notice how members answer the questions. If they get uptight about discussing any of them, you may look for a taboo. ("Mother didn't have an emotional problem; she had bad glands that made her sleep fifteen hours a day.") Look for the openness intra family here, too. Do the children know their grandfather was an alcoholic who used to beat up on Grandmother, or has this been a well kept "secret"? Be aware that moving can be traumatic for children, and some adults, too. A move can represent a loss of all former "happiness." The people who suffer most from moving are often those who have no choice about it (usually children), especially when feelings about the move have not been openly and repeatedly discussed among all members.

Family Process Information

    (to parents)
      "Were your parents ever divorced/how many marriages for each?"
      "What were your parents' occupations/were there unemployment problems?"
      "What was your parents' religion?"
      "Have you ever been married before?"
      "Did your relationship change once you had kids?"

Listen for how members answer these questions. Is the information hard to talk about? Are all the facts common knowledge? Old divorces and old religious injunctions can play a part in people's lives forever if the guilt and other negative feelings about them are not dealt with.

Background Information

Dates of births, marriages, and deaths; birth order; and a few questions about the parents' grandparents help you to complete a picture of the family's process. It is significant if the members are unable to answer any one of these questions. Is it information they were never supposed to know for some reason (family secret)? Or are they blocking the information because they can't deal with the feelings? ("My father died in 1964 — no, 1967 — I can't remember.")

Marriage "Contract"

(to parents)
"What attracted you to each other?"

The parents' answers to this question will give you an idea of their marriage and life contract. Most often this will be an unstated agreement between the two.[1] Note if their relationship is based on competitive rivalry or if one strong member is supporting the weaker one, a protection game in which one or both shield the other from the vicissitudes of the outside world. Some contracts work in a mutually beneficial way for both members, other contracts negate growth for one or both members. Sometimes a contract that was fine ten years ago is now irrelevant and needs to be renegotiated between the partners — but first you, and they, need to recognize what the contract is.

DRAW A HOUSE (30 minutes)

Description of Exercise

Have the whole family draw a house together without talking to each other; then indicate in the house, or on the paper, their own individual spaces.

The point of this exercise is to see how the family communicates, negotiates, and generally interacts together during an active project without any talking among members. And to see from the picture they draw the kind of image they have of their living space and how each individual sees h/self in relationship to that living space. For all of our families, intentionally interacting nonverbally was a new experience. Some found it difficult, most found it fun, all said they learned something about their families — "We talk too much," "Mother controls what goes on at home," "Wow, we all have a different idea of how our house could be."

---

[1]"A couple's behavior may be governed by . . . covert agreements. . . . When the contracts work the marriage is a happy one. Trouble occurs when these contracts are mutually contradictory or impossible to fulfill." Helen Singer Kaplan, *The New Sex Therapy* (New York: Brunner/Mazel, 1974), p. 162.

Equipment

Tape recorder
A large piece of paper (we used 3' x 6'), a box of crayons, and enough floor space so the family can move freely around the paper

Directions to the Family

"This is a nonverbal exercise — that means no talking to each other or to me. I'd like you to use these crayons and this paper to draw a house together for your family. You have ten minutes." You may reassure them that this is not an art contest, just an exercise. Some families will say, "Before we start we want to know whether you want us to draw our house, our old house, or dream house?" You can point out that a pre-drawing agreement will negate the process of nonverbal communication. Be careful not to respond to complaints or jokes the family might make about the no-talking rule. Simply repeat the directions if you have to. An additional direction may be necessary. If after seven minutes the members have not started to put themselves in the drawing, say: "Now I'd like you each to put yourselves in the drawing." When the drawing period is over ask each member, "What house were you drawing?" Ask the whole family, "Were there surprises or were all of you aware what house you were drawing together?" We found it took about thirty minutes to complete the entire exercise — including grappling with paper and crayons, giving directions, the ten-minute drawing period, questions afterward, and putting away materials.

Directions for Interviewer

How to Write Down Nonverbal Interactions. While the family is drawing, your job is to jot down all of their nonverbal interactions: *positive touching, negative touching, positive interacting, negative interacting, family working all together, rearrangements of family position, distractions, separating actions, power behavior, lonerism.*

Write the interactions in the sequence in which they occur, using the initials of the people involved in each interaction and a symbol for each kind of interaction. A sample of how we took these notes is on page 135, "Nonverbal Notes."

Writing Down Drawing Dynamics. You will need to find out who wrote which messages (if any) and who drew which parts of the house. If you are working with a co-interviewer, he/she can jot down the drawing Dynamics sequentially while you are noting the nonverbal interactions. If you are working solo, you will have to *question the family on what happened* after they have finished drawing. A sample of how we took these notes is on page 137–138, "Drawing Notes."

ASSESSING DRAW A HOUSE

Write down your assessment scores and comments on the sheets provided in the Kit.

If you wish to use our scoring system for the exercise see Appendix 2.

Skills

1. *Openness Intra Family.* The members' physical contact with each other — how much they touch each other, both positively (tp) and negatively (tn) — patting, pushing, punching, snuggling, tapping for attention.

2. *Positive Contact with Each Other.* Positive physical contact (tp). All other positive interactions like eye contact, smiling, nodding, laughing, beckoning (p).

3. *Ability to Play.* The general mood of the family while drawing — this can vary from hilarious to angry or gloomy.
The final picture: is the space freely filled or is the drawing confined to the center or to one corner? Is the house clear and colorful, full of imagination and invention or is it a sketchy gray outline?

4. *Ability to Get What You Want.* The wholeness and togetherness of the house in the final drawing. Is it all in one perspective — is it in fact one house or several different ones? Has the family agreed by written or nonverbal messages to cooperate on the drawing? Do they all work together on any part of it, or do they always draw separately or in subgroups? Do any members stay always alone, in a vacuum? Do any members place themselves (in the drawing) only outside the house? Perhaps the family system does not work for them.

5. *Accepting Individual Differences.* Does each member indicate h/self clearly on the paper either by writing a name or initials, drawing a portrait, or staking out in some way a separate space such as a bedroom, or hobby area? While the family is drawing, are the individuals able to change position freely around the paper, or are they locked into one immobile mass?

6. *Limit Setting.* Are the members able, when necessary, to keep others from taking over their private space, the general space, or from distracting the group from the project?

7. *Openness to the Outside.* In the final drawing, does it look as if people can get both into and out of the house? Are there doors or windows? Is there an outdoors with perhaps a driveway or sidewalk, cars, bikes, or other transportation?

Negative Mechanisms

1. *Speaking for Others.* The number of times any members take over other people's spaces, draw others, or others' spaces in the drawing (e.g., in our notes you'll see Mary draws Suzy's mess in Suzy's room; Suzy puts Mary in the front doorway).

2. *Putdowns.* The number of spoken and written putdowns (e.g., the message from Suzy to Billy — "yech!"). To these, add the number of negative nonverbal interactions from your notes: negative touching (tn) such as pushing, grabbing, slapping; and other negative interactions (n) such as scowling, "go away" gestures and signals and body language like back turning.

3. Other Negative Mechanisms most likely to occur in the House Drawing are: *distractions,* somebody lying on the paper so nobody else can draw; *giving orders,* one member directing traffic by means of written messages, gestures, or physical pushing; "I won't play," a member who refuses to participate; *placating,* a member cajoling another into "enjoying" the game.

Family Dynamics

1. Assumptions. Are members surprised after the drawing to find that they have not only guessed wrong about what house others were drawing, but that they have acted on their wrong guesses? "Oh, I thought you started to draw our own house, so I continued it for you. I didn't know you wanted it to be a castle on the Rhine."

2. Sexism. Is the family in the drawing locked into sex roles, e.g., females in the kitchen, males by the fireplace? While drawing do males do the general outline, particularly the roof, do females put curtains and furniture in the house?

3. Power. Who takes charge of the messages or the drawing and/or who receives most of the nonverbal interactions in the family — the "unapproachable" one? The "sick" one? The "comforter"? And/or who starts more interactions than anyone else?

4. Boundaries. Family boundaries: are the boundary outlines of the house hazy or clear, impregnable or with openings? Individual boundaries: note which members are clearly and carefully defined, and which are hazy, unconnected to the house, or drawn only in communal living spaces with no privacy.

5. Family Alliances. Sometimes a never verbalized family lineup will appear both in the final drawing and in the way the family positions itself and interacts while drawing, two children separating mother and father, mother and daughters together, father and sons together.

Chapter 7

Interview 2

ROLE CARD GAME
FAMILY PROBLEMS
ASKING FOR WHAT YOU WANT
FAMILY BONANZA

ROLE CARD GAME (30 minutes)

Description of Exercises

Have the members, without talking, pick out cards (listed below) for themselves, and for each other. The cards describe household job roles during dinner-evening-bedtime, and certain kinds of interaction roles. Each member has a chance to state agreement or disagreement about the accuracy of each card for each person in the family, and a chance at the end to reject cards he/she does not want to keep.

Job Roles (24)

Household Organizer	Drink Maker	Gives Small Kids Baths
Food Shopper	Cook	Puts Kids to Bed
Meal Planner	Table Setter	Outdoor Worker
Floor Washer	Table Clearer	Holiday Manager
Big Filthy Jobs	Unloads the Dishwasher	Rule Maker
Errand Runner	Washes Dishes	Disciplinarian
Fixer	After Meal Kitchen Cleanup	Responsible for Everything
Cleans up after Snacks	Pet Feeder	
	Trash Person	

Interaction Roles (12)

Positive	*Negative*
Truthteller	Blamer
Helpful One	Placater
Understanding One	Computer
Creative One	Lone Wolf
Happy Person	Distracter
Negotiator	Victim

The point of this exercise is to find out, in a nonthreatening card game setting, how the members see themselves and each other in terms of job and interaction roles. You will look for discrepancies between how a member sees h/self and others see him/her. You will see how household jobs are distributed, and whether all members are satisfied with that distribution. Also, you will observe the family interacting in a nonverbal situation with a great deal of structure (unlike the House Drawing). Of the families we interviewed, the more verbally oriented ones really enjoyed playing this game — and went on to invent more "roles" for one another after the interview, expanding their learning experience.

Equipment

Tape recorder
36 role cards (We cut 4″ x 6″ file cards into thirds to make 4″ x 2″ cards, and printed one role on each card.)
A piece of paper, a pencil, and an elastic for each member
A table around which the whole family can comfortably sit (If you don't have one, use the floor.)

Directions to the Family

Seat the family around a table and give each member a piece of paper with his/her name on it and a pencil. "I am going to lay out a bunch of cards. I'd like each of you to pick up the cards that are accurate for you and lay them in front of you on the table so that others can see them. If someone picks up a card you feel belongs to you, write it on the paper in front of you — this isn't a contest to see who can get the most cards." Lay out the cards while saying, "Please wait till everybody has a chance to see all the cards before you pick them up." Add: "This is going to be a nonverbal game — that means no talking. If you don't know the meaning of a card, please ask me, not each other. These cards are not just for your family, so all cards do not have to be picked up."

When you think each person in the family is satisfied with the role cards he/she has picked or written on the paper, give the next direction: "Now I'd like you, one at a time, first to check out whether your own cards are all accurate for you. Next, check out each other person's cards. Say, into the tape recorder, if you think a card they have is not accurate for them ('Mother, I don't think you're an Errand Runner'). Also say, into the tape recorder, if you think a card you or someone else has picked or a card that is left over belongs to them ('Mother, I think you are a Disciplinarian')." As the interviewer, you may have to ask here, "Are you taking Disciplinarian away from your dad or are you saying that it's accurate for both your mother and dad?"

The next direction: "If someone gives you a card that you think is wrong for you, say, into the tape recorder, "I think Disciplinarian is wrong for me," then put the card into a separate 'wrong' pile, or write it on your paper as 'wrong' if somebody else already has possession of the card."

When each person has had a turn to check out his/her opinion of each other's cards, give the final direction: "Now is your chance to get rid of any roles you do not like, even though they may be correct for you. Discard the role onto the center of the table. Go one at a time, and say what you are doing into the tape recorder. For example, 'I, Mary, am throwing out Floor Washer, Washes Dishes, Cleans up after Snacks, After Meal Kitchen Cleanup, Big Filthy Jobs, Unloads Dishwasher, and Blamer.' "

When each member has had a chance to throw out unwanted roles, ask them each to put an elastic around the roles they've kept and the paper on which they've written roles. These will be important to you for scoring. Keep them separate, and make sure their names are on them.

Last, as you are cleaning up, ask each member to answer the question "Do you have any fun together at dinner and in the evening?" Their answers will be an indication of the family's *ability to play* (see page 79).

Directions for Interviewer

Children. You'll have to help young or nonreading children with this game by playing it with them — in their chair, so to speak. Read each card to them. Allow them to choose what belongs to them — even if they take every single card, or no cards. Also help them check out the others' cards: "Do you think your mother is a Cook?" and allow them to say yes or no. Let them decide whether to keep cards that others want to give them. For the discards, ask them, "Do you want to be a Fixer, a Cook?" etc., and let them say yes or no. You may feel some children in the family are too young to understand the game. (Our youngest participant was five and he did fine; we decided not to include two- and three-year-old brothers in a family we interviewed.) You can explain to little children that you're going to do a card game with their family that may not be too interesting to them; that they're welcome to watch the family play if they'd like. You can offer them crayons and paper and ask if they'd rather draw a picture of their family eating dinner, Mother or Father coming home from work, their bedtime, or whatever you think is relevant.

If small children are being left out of the role game, or if someone is unavoidably absent, add to your directions to the family: "After you have each chosen your cards, please agree among you which cards Jimmy would pick for himself," (probably very few). When the members are going around the table checking each other's accuracy, have each include Jimmy: "I think Jimmy is [*or* is not] a Victim." During the discards have the family agree which cards, if any, Jimmy might discard: "We don't think he wants to be a Victim."

ASSESSING THE ROLE CARD GAME

Write down your assessment scores and comments on the sheets provided in the Kit.

If you wish to use our scoring system for the exercise, see Appendix 2.

Skills

1. *Shared Facts, Meanings, Values.* Agreement among family members about the roles all pick for themselves and each other. Are most roles accurate — or are many "wrong" or "not belong"? Are there discrepancies between how a member sees h/self and others in the family see him/her?

2. *Responsibility.* Look for job sharing, and parents modeling and teaching job sharing to the children. What kinds of jobs do the various members pick?

3. *Positive Contact with Each Other.* Members giving each other positive roles during the game.

4. *Ability to Play.* In answer to your question "Do you have any fun together at dinner and in the evening," get a sense of the kind of fun that occurs, and whether all members agree that it is fun. One of our families patently enjoyed dinner as a time to "sharpen their wits" — they all agreed there was warmth, much laughing and joking. In another family, Father thought dinner was fun because he could share what happened at the office; Daughter thought it was a "bore." A third family used dinner as a time to carry out family fights.

5. *Accepting Individual Differences.* Is it possible for members to be different from one another, or to change the accepted image of themselves? Members' ability and willingness to reject roles they do not want measure the family system's permission for members to be different and to change.

6. *Internally Chosen Roles.* Do family members tend to think of themselves positively, or do some members get singled out by

the family as being the "bad" one, or the one who placates, distracts or blames?

Negative Mechanisms

1. Putdowns. The negative interaction roles the family members give to one another, along with any putdowns you hear as you listen to the tape.

2. Self-Putdowns. The negative interaction roles members choose for themselves, along with any spoken self-putdowns.

3. Other Negative Mechanisms to watch for are *unnecessary questions* and *inappropriate jokes*. If there is joking or repeated questioning about the meaning of any of the role cards this may indicate a family trouble spot. Note which cards give trouble: "What does Negotiator mean again?" or "Ha, ha, Dad, you're the Truthteller, yeah, yeah!" Note also who is doing the asking or joking — is it consistently one person using those Mechanisms for defense or anger, or does the whole family join in? Suzy, for example, uses naive questions as a way of maintaining her baby position in the Smith family.

Family Dynamics

1. Sexism. Are the jobs divided along traditional sex lines? That is, do only the females do "women's work" — organizing, planning, and kitchen chores; do only the males do "men's work" — outdoor jobs, pet feeding, taking out the trash, drink making? Does the husband/father automatically pick up Rule Maker and Disciplinarian? Do either or both adults feel Responsible for Everything, indicating that they feel burdened, with no one to help share that burden? Or can members cross traditional sex lines in terms of household jobs — share what needs to be done without prejudice as to which sex is supposed to do which set of jobs?

2. Scapegoating. If anyone picks or is given the Victim card, look carefully to see if that person is being scapegoated by the family. There are three basic indexes of scapegoating in the Role Card Game: a) other members giving Victim to the scapegoat, or unanimously agreeing that the Victim card is accurate if he/she has picked it for h/self; b) other members giving the scapegoat only negative interaction roles, never positive ones; c) other members taking away positive roles and also job roles the scapegoat has picked for h/self — saying, in effect, "Those don't belong to you, you don't do anything good around here." When all three of these elements are combined, you will see a family energy behind what's happening, as we did in one of our families where one child was clearly being singled out as a scapegoat. There was hostility in the voices of the other children as each one in turn repeatedly doled out the negative roles and said the positive ones did not belong. While the parents did not display hostility so overtly, they, too, gave only negative roles and took away positive ones, and by nonverbal means (e.g., the mother stroking the little sister's back as she shouted at the scapegoat) sanctioned and fully colluded in the family's scapegoating behavior.

An interesting phenomenon in families is the "White Knight" — a sort of through-the-looking-glass opposite of the scapegoat, — that is, a member upon whom all others dump only good qualities.[1] The burden the White Knight carries around is that he/she has to be good, right, responsible, perfect, in order to get rewards from, or even belong to, the family system. He/she is never permitted by the family or h/self to show any negative feelings. Although we did not uncover a true White Knight in any of our families, we surmise that the Role Card Game will reveal one if a family repeatedly and energetically loads one member with only positive roles, and indicates that that member willingly does almost all household jobs — in fact, rescues other members from having to do them.

3. Power. The Role Card Game will add to what you have started to learn in Draw a House about the family's power struc-

[1]Carl A. Whitaker, from a workshop, Pine Manor Junior College, Brookline, Massachusetts: Human Resources Institute, April 19, 1974.

ture (or lack of one). Look for who does most jobs, who "takes charge" of the game by giving or taking away a great many roles from others, and who receives a great many roles from others (i.e., receives a lot of attention). Chances are that person or those people wield power in the family.

4. Family Alliances. Another adjunct to the information you have noted in Draw a House. Look for pairing or family lineups. Who shares jobs with whom? Do two people play against each other — that is, give many roles back and forth? Does one subgroup gang up on another subgroup to lay on negative roles?

5. Anger. The question of household jobs is a good one for getting families into some anger. Listen for verbal anger like "You never do a damned thing around the house." Watch for people taking job roles away from others and laying on negative roles (sibling anger shows up here between Suzy and Billy). Sometimes the anger is palpable (they'll slap the cards down, their voice will sound tense, angry). Sometimes it's subtle or masked (a forced smile, or avoidance of eye contact with another person). Sometimes the anger may be merely a bad vibe you feel in the room during the game. Even that is noteworthy.

6. Emotional Support. If a family shares jobs pretty equally, gives only positive roles to each other, and takes away only negative roles from one another, they are demonstrating mutual emotional support. Note the warmth, caring, and validating that you feel in the family from the members' smiles, eye contact, and general attentiveness to one another. You will feel good vibes in the room.

7. Hidden Agenda. Underground conflicts, unspoken in the family, about who a person really is and what he/she needs from others, may show up in the role cards. See Billy choosing Lone Wolf. Both parents say this card does not belong to him. They believe him to be close to them; he is a teenager struggling to get out of the family. The family's hidden agenda is that struggle.

Nonverbal Notes. Note how the family plays the game. Is their mood up or down; is there shrieking, card grabbing, anger, or hilarity; or is there organization and calm? Do people arrange their cards so that others can read them or do they mess, hoard, hide, or drop them on the floor? Mary, who complains elsewhere about Suzy's mess, lays her own cards out so messily that no one else can tell what she's chosen.

FAMILY PROBLEMS (20 minutes)

Description of Exercise

Have each member write what he/she considers to be the biggest problem in the family. Then ask the members to discuss together the problems in their family.

The point of this exercise is to find out what the individuals in the family think their problems are and how direct and open they are about dealing with them. Again, you will be watching for the family's process — how they interact as they talk about their problems. This is a particularly good chance to watch the individuals' nonverbal behavior to see if it matches the content of what they are saying.

Equipment

Tape recorder
Pencil and one card for each family member (Write people's names on the cards, or ask them to, so you can identify them later.)

Directions to the Family

"Every family has problems, some bigger than others. I'd like each of you to write down on your cards what you think is the bigest problem in your family. Then hand the cards to me. I won't show them to anyone else in the family. Please don't talk to each other while you're writing." This should take the family about five minutes — you can remind them of the time if they look as if they are going to take more. Be sure to enforce the no-talking rule if the family starts to compare notes during the writing. When everyone has handed you the cards, say: "Now I'd like you all to discuss the problems in your family for ten or fifteen minutes. Each person try to respond to each problem."

Directions for Interviewer

Your main job here is to watch and listen. Beware of intervening in the discussion, tempting though it might be. We took careful notes on individuals' nonverbal behavior while they and other members were talking and found the notes really helpful when we listened later to the tape.

Children. You will have to help children who can't write with this exercise. When you give the writing direction, say: "Jimmy, I'll help you write down the problem you think is biggest in the family. Come on over here with me." Ask him to whisper to you what he thinks is the problem and write down whatever he says, without judging or editing in any way. Read it back to him to make sure he agrees that what you have written is what he thinks. He may not want to tell you anything. Don't push. You are helping with the writing only so that another family member won't do it.

ASSESSING FAMILY PROBLEMS

Write down your assessment scores and comments on the sheets provided in the Kit.

If you wish to use our scoring system for this exercise, see Appendix 2.

Skills

1. *Risk Taking.* Is each of the members able to state a serious problem that directly involves family feelings?

2. *Openness intra Family.* Do family members respond to the stated problems in a way that carries the discussion forward in a

problem-solving direction? Do they deal with the feeling part of the problems as well as the logistical part? In particular, are members allowed to express negative feelings without someone else putting the feelings down, evading them, or trying to make the feelings go away? Look here for a sharing among members about the real nature of the problems.

3. *Openness to the Outside.* Are members able to write a serious problem on a card, which will be read by you, the outside observer?

Negative Mechanisms

The whole gamut of family Negative Mechanisms may show up here, but we found the following to be most prevalent in Family Problems:

1. *Evasions.* Do members change the subject, space off, or otherwise avoid directly dealing with their own or others' problems or feelings?

2. *Denials.* "I never said that" when the speaker just did. "The problem is that Dad's never home — but that doesn't bother *me*." "There *are* no problems in this family." All of these constitute denials — of fact or of feelings.

3. *Double Messages.* Do members state their problems or respond to others' problems in a conflicted, "double" way: "Of course you can paint your room that ugly blue, I don't care"?

4. *Speaking for Others.* Do members state another member's problem, or feelings about a problem instead of allowing him/her to do so for h/self.

5. *Placating.* "Now, now, you two," says John to Mary and Suzy who are arguing, "It's not that bad . . . ."

6. *Blaming.* Do members fault each other, or the whole family, rather than express their own negative feelings about a problem? The response to a blame is almost certain to be some kind of self-defense, which makes any real, open, problem-solving discussion impossible; e.g., Mary, in response to Suzy's blaming

request for "more privileges," responds with another blame: "It's your own fault you don't get privileges. You want too much."

7. Inappropriate Jokes. Individuals, or the whole family, may get into elaborate or hilarious joking about family problems. Even though the family may seem quite jolly throughout the problem discussion, listen to hear if the jokes have a cutting edge, are aimed at someone in the family, or stop open discussion of feelings, or even of logistics, about the problem.

8. Putdowns. Suzy responds to the problem Billy has written down with a putdown: "You never have any trouble, you're such a Momma's boy."

9. Self-Putdowns. "The problem I wrote down isn't important...."

Family Dynamics

1. Collusions. Is there an unspoken agreement among two or more members not to bring up or discuss a certain problem, or to divert feelings by evading, joking, denying, or discussing "nonproblems"? Such a collusion may be subtle, and you may become aware of it only when listening to the discussion on tape. A clever family, colluding not to discuss a problem, can put on a wonderful outward show of earnest concern while never dealing with the realities of the problem.

2. Secrets, Myths, Taboos. A secret that Mother drinks; a myth that Father rules the family; a taboo about discussing Sister's sexual relationship with her boyfriend — somebody may let the family cat out of the bag during this exercise.

3. Hidden Agenda. A member may state a problem that sounds real enough ("The children won't tell me their plans"), but that statement may be hiding a parent's real agenda: "I have no self-confidence, and I'm scared that if my children do something bad, the neighbors will think I'm a bad parent and an unworthy person." Hidden agendas often turn up in the form of complaints or blames, and are often responded to defensively. Check out — when you hear this sort of dialogue — whether it is masking some real, emotional content — old anger, fear, loneliness.

4. *Assumption Making.* "You've been angry at me ever since I changed jobs," Father may say (to Mother) as the problem. "I can't have a dog so I spend all my time at my friend's house," says ten-year-old Tommy, having never asked for a dog. Statements like these, about what someone else feels or thinks, if they have never been checked out with the other person, are assumptions.

5. *Scapegoating.* Do members single out one member as being the problem, or the cause of the family problems? See Suzy, page 148, "Content of Cards." She comes close to being a scapegoat, but John will not join in.

6. *Death.* If a death is mentioned as part of a problem, note all the members' reactions to determine whether the family deals openly with death or is unable to deal with feelings about death, grief, and loss. Be aware that for a child or even an adult the death of an animal may be of prime significance.

7. *Anger.* Is there hidden or open anger during this exercise? Note nonverbal behavior like fist clenching, writhing, teeth grinding as well as verbal blaming, complaining, and shouting.

Nonverbal Notes. Look for defensive nonverbal behavior; squirming, arms crossed over chest, leaving the room on whatever pretext, knocking the lamp over.... Also look for whether a person's nonverbal behavior matches the content of the problem he/she is talking about. For instance, a member may say with a calm smile "I don't feel anybody listens to me around here." He/she may be feeling really angry or sad, but does not show it.

ASKING FOR WHAT YOU WANT (30 minutes)

Description of Exercise

Have each member write on a card what they want most from each other member of the family, and what they think each other member wants from them. Then have each member directly ask all other members for what they want most from them, without referring to the cards. After that have each member write on another card what each person asked them for, whether or not they think they can give it to that person, and whether or not they think they can get what they asked for from that person.

The point of this exercise is to see if the individuals in the family can be honest about their wants and needs, can communicate them directly to each other, and can have them heard and understood. You will be watching here as much for the family's communication process as for what the individuals' needs are. Most of our families found this exercise difficult or "nerve-racking" because it was a new experience for them to honestly identify their wants/needs, and to ask directly for what they want. Despite (or because of) the difficulty, these families found the exercise made an impact on them — gave them permission to state their needs outright instead of hinting around, wishing others could read their mind, or assuming they had to go without. In one family there was a real breakthrough in which the father was able to hear for the first time from his sons that they wanted a real relationship with him, which his continual advice-giving behavior did not permit. The sons risked talking directly about their needs; the father was able to understand that they wanted to know him better and not simply receive paternal advice.

Equipment

Tape recorder

A pencil and two cards for each member: a Want Card and a Question Card. Prepare the cards beforehand, following the sample below. (Also see pages 152–154.)

Want Card: Side 1
JOHN
I want from Mary:
I want from Billy:
I want from Suzy:

Want Card: Side 2
JOHN
Mary wants from me:
Billy wants from me:
Suzy wants from me:

Question Card

JOHN	What did each person ask you for?	Do you think you can give it to them?	Do you think you can get what you asked for from them?
MARY			
BILLY			
SUZY			

Directions to the Family

(Hand out the Want Cards.)

"I'd like you each to write down on these cards what you want most for yourself from each person in the family. Next, write down what you think each person wants from you. Please don't talk to each other." (This should take about five minutes. You may have to jog an individual who is having a hard time thinking of "anything.")

(Gather the Want Cards.)

"Now I'd like each of you to ask each person in the family directly for what you want most from each of them for yourself.

Everybody please try to respond. You can be brief — this should take about one minute per transaction." At this point we demonstrated asking and responding more or less like this: Gina: "What I want most from you, Anne, is to let me know when you're going to be late, so that I know whether to wait for you or to start working without you on our write-ups." Anne: "I hear you say you need better communication from me about time. When I'm going to be late, I'll give you a call so you'll be able to plan your workday." When you have a co-interviewer, you can demonstrate with each other. (It rings truer if you use a real issue between you.)

When each member has had a chance to ask for something from each other member, hand out the Question Cards. "Each of you please fill out these cards — quickly — with no talking or checking out with each other. What did each person ask you for? Do you think you can give it to him or her? Do you think you can get what you asked for from each of them?" (Gather the cards when everyone is through — it should take about five minutes to fill them out.)

Directions for Interviewer

As in Family Problems, watch and listen closely for how the family interacts. Notes on nonverbal behavior — individual and interactions — will be helpful when you listen to the taped verbal interactions.

Some people will have a hard time responding in this exercise when they are asked for something. If they do not respond, score them for an evasion, as directed on page 150.

Children. With children who can't write, you'll have to help them as you did in Family Problems. Read the directions on the cards and ask them to whisper answers to you. Write their answers on the cards and check to see if you have written the answers accurately. Be sure, during the oral part of the exercise, not to speak for them. Let tham ask and respond for themselves.

ASSESSING ASKING FOR WHAT YOU WANT

Write down your assessment scores and comments on the sheets provided in the Kit.

If you wish to use our scoring system for this exercise, see Appendix 2.

Skills

1. *Straight Talking/Responding.* Are members clear about what they are asking for from each other? Are they clear in the way they respond to each other? Or do they change their minds midstream to avoid direct contact with one another? Billy says to Mary, "I want not to be so close to you. I need to grow up and be getting ready to leave for college. I feel like I'm in a box sometimes." That's straight talking.

2. *Listening.* Do members hear what others ask them for, or do they mishear or "forget"?

3. *Risk Taking.* Do members risk asking each other directly for something for *themselves?* "I would like you to spend more time with me, Mother"; Father, I'd like you to hug me sometimes." Examples of nonrequests for self would be: "Janie, I'd like you to become a doctor," or "Dad, I'd like you to pay more attention to Charlie." The feeling self is left out of these last requests, therefore there is no real risk involved in hearing the answer.

4. *Positive Contact with Each Other.* Do members' responses to each other acknowledge each others' feelings — either by a direct affirmative "Yes, I'll be glad to do that for you" or by a direct understanding of the feelings involved, even if it is impossible to give the thing asked for: "No, Charlie, I don't want to give you my new bathrobe, but you can wear it sometimes if you like"?

5. *Ability to Get What You Want.* Are members realistic about what they think they can get from one another? John, for example, wants, and thinks he can get, from Mary, "sympathy for

Suzy," although Mary laughed when he asked her. He is not being entirely realistic here. He is realistic, however, in thinking that he can get "friendship" from Billy.

Negative Mechanisms

1. Evasions. Inability to verbalize the wants written on the Want Card; or inability to respond verbally, or on the Question Card, to another's request (e.g., Suzy does not ask for anything from John on her card, and does not orally respond to Billy's request). Also, patently noncommittal requests and responses — either spoken or on the cards.

2. Putdowns. Using requests as a vehicle to ask people to stop bad behavior. Mary says to Suzy, "Stop being a pain." Also note any putdowns in response to requests (e.g., "No, you can't use my baseball cards, Dummy, you always mess stuff up.")

3. Denials. Suzy (to Mary): "I wish you wouldn't say 'No' so often." Mary: "I don't say 'No.' I don't know what you mean."

Family Dynamics

1. Hidden Agenda. If members' spoken requests and responses are not the same as their written requests and responses (i.e., *straight talking*), look for a possible hidden agenda. Do members ask for what they really want, or do they hide their wants and/or give double messages about them. Suzy writes to Billy, "I want to use your things." She knows Billy won't let her, since he constantly complains about it. Her hidden agenda may be: "I want more attention from Billy."

2. Assumption Making. Any wide discrepancy between what members say they want from one another and what the others have guessed and written in on the "want cards" may constitute an assumption. If, as with Suzy and John, John writes that she wants "fatherliness" from him, and Suzy says nothing, he has made an assumption. Also, Billy writes and says that he wants more distance from his mother. Mary assumes he wants "more support" and maintains she knows the real truth when she writes on her Question Card that Billy wants "approval" from her.

3. Anger. If you hear verbal anger, or see nonverbal anger, note who is angry at whom.

4. Emotional Support. Note the kinds of validating between the members, mentioning names. Note direct warmth, such as one member's encouraging another verbally and with smiles and nods to ask him/her for something.

5. Sex. Note if partners use this exercise to express satisfaction or dissatisfaction about their sexual relationship. One woman wrote that she wanted a "weekend away" with her husband, explaining later that they had never left the children in twelve years of marriage.

Nonverbal Notes. Note the tension level in the room while the family is writing the Want Cards. If it is high — if there is much fidgeting, spacing off, difficulty in completing the cards — you have a clue that the direct asking is going to be very hard for the family. While the family is asking each other, watch to see which individuals look closed off (arms folded, lips pursed, body twisted) and which look relaxed and open. Are any members "unapproachable"? Is it because they are closed to hearing the requests, or is it that the requests and nonverbal approaches are tentative or full of double messages? Look here specifically for members touching points of body pain — rubbing the back of the neck, clutching hands over the stomach. It may be so painful to ask for anything that the member being asked shuts out the request in order to shut out noticing, and having to respond to, the pain.

> I want it
> I get it
> therefore I am good
>
> I want it
> I don't get it
> Therefore I am bad

I am bad
> because I didn't get it

I am bad
> because I wanted what I didn't get

I must take care
> to get what I want
> and want what I get
> and not get what I don't want[2]

FAMILY BONANZA (30 minutes)

Description of Exercise

Give the family a "windfall check" in the amount of their total yearly income. Ask the members to write down how each would like the family to spend the money; then ask members to negotiate together how the family will spend the money, each trying to get what he/she wants.

The point of this exercise is to see how the family negotiates when presented money and the prospect of pleasure. Can members communicate directly with one another? Can they get what they want individually and as a family? Are they imaginative and open to change? Do parents model good negotiating for the children? Is the family able to make a decision? Again, you will be watching and listening for the family's process — how they play the game — as well as for what they decide to spend the money on. Some families thought this game was fun — felt free about fantasizing how to spend large sums, laughed a lot, felt "up" when the game was over. For others it brought up old money problems, arguments, or taboos. They found the game difficult, depressing, and had trouble negotiating. One family concluded that "money cannot buy happiness," so they agreed not to make any decisions about it at all and ended up feeling angry at us for asking them to play the game.

[2] R. D. Laing, *Knots* (New York: Pantheon, 1970), p. 38.

Equipment

Tape recorder.

A "check" for the yearly family income (we used a file card and wrote on it "$25,000 [or whatever the family's income was] from your rich uncle.")

Pencils and cards for each member (write member's names on the cards for later identification, or ask them to.)

Directions to the Family

Hand out pencils and cards to each member. Place the "check" face down at a more or less equal distance from all members. "I'm giving your family a check. I'd like each of you to think privately, without talking, about how you would like your family to spend the money, and write it on the cards."

When the family has finished writing, say: "You may keep your cards during this exercise. First, each of you say how you'd like to spend the money. Then I'd like the whole family to negotiate together how you all will spend the money. Each of you try to get what you want. You have about ten minutes."

If the family has not reached a decision in ten minutes, give them a time limit — "one more minute." When the negotiating time is over, say to the family (whether they have reached a decision or not): "Please write on the back of the check how you will spend the money. Next to each item note how much money you'll spend on it." When this written, say: "Each of you please initial the list if you agree with it." Ask them to hand you all the cards at the end of the game.

Directions for Interviewer

Again, watch closely to see if the family's nonverbal communication matches what you are hearing. Is loud laughing really masking anger, which you can pick up by observing such behavior as fist banging, grimacing, aggressive pointing? Or maybe the family is really having fun. If so, their postures will look open and relaxed, and there will be eye contact and smiles between the members.

Children. If you have to help nonwriting children, do as you did in Family Problems and Asking for What You Want. Have them whisper to you how they'd like to spend the money. Check out with them what you've written on their card. Resist the temptation to negotiate for them. Your job here is to see how the family does on its own — whether it includes a small child in the negotiating or ignores the child; whether people speak for the child or encourage the child to speak for h/self. Watch the child carefully throughout the negotiating. Does he/she actively try to join in, or try to distract the others, or shrink into a corner. A small child's nonverbal behavior here will often tell you a lot about how it feels to live in a particular family.

ASSESSING FAMILY BONANZA

Write down your assessment scores and comments on the sheets provided in the Kit.

If you wish to use our scoring system for this exercise, see Appendix 2.

Skills

1. *Straight Talking/Responding.* Do members negotiate in a decision-making direction, or is their conversation loaded with diversions, jokes, denials, evasions, and other Negative Mechanisms?

2. *Listening.* Do members indicate that they hear each other's wishes?

3. *Negotiating.* We consider negotiating a separate Skill, although we score it as a combination of several other Skills. Are the members able to talk and respond straight, listen to what others say, individually and collectively get what they want, and make a mutual decision? Good negotiating will combine communication, and problem-solving Skills and high family self-esteem.

4. Decision Making. Is the family able to decide, mutually, how they are going to spend the money? Or do some members refuse to agree, or does the entire family agree *not* to decide how to spend it?

5. Responsibility. Do parents and other adults (i.e., aunts, grandfathers, *not* grown children) model straight talking/responding for the children?

6. Ability to Play. Is the family imaginative? Do members have fun with their own and each other's fantasies about how to spend the money?

7. Ability to Get What You Want. Do members get to spend money on what they want? Do members speak up for what they want in a way that others respond to?

8. Accepting Individual Differences. Does each member have at least one wish that is different from every other member's wishes? Is that wish acknowledged in some way by the others? See Suzy negotiating for a yacht: she has a separate wish, but nobody acknowledges it.

9. Openness to the Outside. Is the family receptive to experiment and change — how much does it decide to spend on fantasies? A family that is not open will tend to hoard the money or spend it to get more of what they already have. You may have to make a judgment about the context here. If a family has (in reality) just moved into a new house, they may decide to spend every penny on painting, fixing, plumbing, furnishing the house. You will have to decide, in such a case, whether the family seems stuck in a rut of practicalities, or if their practicality is dictated by a special situation; e.g., the Smiths' summer cabin is their escape place. It seems more of a fantasy than a practical need when they choose to put improvements into it.

Negative Mechanisms

1. Evasion. Listen for evasions particularly when members make noncommittal responses or no responses to others' wishes.

Also, when members oppose, is their opposition direct or do they somehow avoid ever saying a direct "No, I don't like that"?

2. *Denials.* "I never said I wanted to go on the trip to Hawaii" — after the speaker has brought it up, and the family has negotiated about it. Or — "Well, I may have mentioned the trip, but I didn't really like the idea."

3. *Speaking for Others.* "I think Dad wants to get a boat, Mom wants a tennis court, and Janie wants a horse." Terrific, but let Dad, Mom, and Janie speak for themselves. Also listen for members directly negotiating for others' wishes that are not also their own. Supporting another's wishes is warm, validating behavior; actually negotiating for another member who is old enough to do so for h/self is intrusion.

4. *Giving Orders.* "Carl, you write the card — figure out how much money we can spend on a trip — tell the children they can't have motorcycles...." If this is a method any members use in order to negotiate, it will probably show up in this exercise.

5. *Placating.* The placater in the family will have a wonderful time in Family Bonanza. He/she can break up arguments, make sure everyone gets what he/she wants (or if that's impossible, tell all members they really do want what they got), and generally make certain that everybody is happy, happy, happy while negotiating. (See John's "Mechanisms" score of 5, page 164, especially when he placates Suzy and Mary who argue about a cabin addition.)

6. *Putdowns.* These may appar particularly when one member is opposing another's wish. Is the opposition straight ("No, I don't want to go to Hawaii") or is it a putdown ("You're stupid — Hawaii costs too much")? Adults often make remarks like "You don't understand money."

7. *Bribes.* "I'll give each of you kids a quarter to vote my way."

8. *General Complaining, Inappropriate Jokes, Distractions and other Negative Mechanisms.* Note these as you do in the other exercises.

Family Dynamics

1. Collusions. Is there an unspoken agreement not to agree — that is, does all the negotiating lead inevitably to the family's agreeing not to spend the money, not to have fun, or not to play the game? Is there an unspoken agreement to give one person everything?

2. Scapegoating. If there is a scapegoat, he/she will "get" less than the others, may not be supported or even responded to as much as the others, and may not speak up for his/her own wishes. The scapegoat will also receive more putdowns than anyone else.

3. Power. Who gives (and writes) the final word? Who gets everything he/she wants, or substantially more than anyone else? Who gets most support for his/her wishes? Who does much more negotiating than anyone else? If that person opposes, do others give up? Any of these point to the power figure in the family.

4. Family Alliances. Who is supportive to whom? Who opposes whom? Add this information to any you may have from the House Drawing and the Role Card Game.

5. Money. You will find out in this exercise, if you haven't before, whether there are taboos about dealing with money. If a family does not enjoy the exercise and gets uptight during the negotiating, ask yourself (and the family) if the subject of money triggers old, bad feelings. Who is the real money handler, and how do others feel about that?

6. Hidden Agenda. If members space off, suddenly change the subject, or start talking nonsense in the course of negotiating, you can suspect a hidden agenda.

7. Nonverbal Notes. This exercise tends to be fun for many families. Look for positive interactions between people — laughing, joking, pleased looks. In other families the subject of money brings out feelings of anger or competition. Parents reject what each other wants with putdown gestures, looks of disgust or contempt. Children who are poked fun at, or not heard, begin to look hurt or depressed. Sibling competition leaves some children sulking. You may see looks of surprise as someone reveals a secret fantasy.

Chapter 8
Deciding Whether You Can Work with a Family

The task now, before you go into the third interview, is to make a clear decision about whether or not you can productively work with the family. You will have the sheets filled out to help you assess the family, and your relationship to them. The question is "Can this family and I work together to learn the Skills the family wants to learn?" Implicit in the question are other assessment questions, some of which you can answer alone; some you will explore during the third interview.

ASSESSING THE FAMILY

If you have filled out the sheets as you have gone along, you will know the family's average Skills score. If you will turn to the filled-in sheets for the Smith family in Appendix 3, you will see that their overall average is 3.5 in Skills. In the four major areas they vary from 3.75 to 3.15. Although the Smith family has several areas that need work, they are not an unhealthy family. In fact, we judged Family A, on whom we based them, to be our healthiest family. Family A had the highest Skills scores, a very low score in Negative Mechanisms on Table 1 (Appendix), and seemed to engage in the fewest dysfunctional Family Dynamics. Our clinical view of this family coincided with these findings.

We have, for purposes of this book, exaggerated their difficulties, added some from other families, changed the sex and number of the children, but the general style of the family remains. And the real Family A and the fictitious Smiths would both be families who would benefit rapidly from working on their problems in family therapy. If you have a family in this general range, we feel the family will not be difficult. As families score lower on the scale, of course, they will require greater expertise.

ASSESSING YOURSELF

The interviewer next has to honestly assess h/self in relation to the family. Are you comfortable with the family? Do you have a bias which will prevent therapy? Does the family seem too much like your own family of origin or present one; that is, are their unresolved problems similar to those remaining unresolved in your own life? If you feel the emotional atmosphere will not start out charged with your own problems or negative feelings about the family, your next question will be: "Can I?"

Since this book was designed in part to give guidelines for lay therapists, we have gone over the scores of the families we interviewed with the skills of lay therapists in mind. Looking at the scores our families had, we feel that overall scores of lower than 2 would indicate difficulties beyond the skills of the lay therapist. In Appendix 1, "Scoring and Numbers," we talk about this in some detail. You, however, must decide what your own chances of success will be with any given family with any score. We are hoping, with this book, to help you avoid biting off more than you can chew. As a guideline about what number is relevant for you, perhaps you can think about families you have succeeded and failed with in terms of the kind of scores you think they might have had using this system.

MUTUAL GOALS

Finally, you'll need to think about the family's stated goals. Are they goals you will feel comfortable working with — or not what you have in mind at all? There has to be a real contract between you and the family, and you have to honestly decide on your part that their goals are acceptable to you, even though you may have some additional ones of your own, which you will want to mention. If the parents' goal, for example, is to make the son go to medical school like his father, you may have to tell the family you cannot share that goal, but you can certainly help them communicate better about the son's decision. If the family's goal is to keep the marriage together, and keeping marriages together is not a goal of yours,[1] you will need to tell them that. Do you have values or standards you feel you need to teach all families? Some, such as open communication, may be valid in your role as therapist with them. But some may be part of your own moral, cultural, or psychic upbringing and not at all the goals of the family.[2] If you can't abandon those in good conscience, you will be better working only with families who share those values and standards. Families come to you for help — not reform. So think hard about your goals and about the family goals and where they differ. Be honest.

---

[1] John Warkentin and Carl A. Whitaker, "The Secret Agenda of the Therapist Doing Couples Therapy," *Family Therapy and Disturbed Families* (Palo Alto, Calif.: Science and Behavior Books, 1967).
[2] Rollo May, *The Art of Counseling* (Nashville, Tenn.: Abingdon Press, 1967).

Chapter 9

Interview 3

INTERVIEWER HOMEWORK — PREPARING THE FEEDBACK

You have completed the first two interviews, and have evaluated the family. That is, you have filled out the History Taking forms, scored the family for Skills in each exercise, scored all their Negative Mechanisms with notes about their significance, noted the Family Dynamics you see blocking family growth, and noted the nonverbal behavior. You know the family well, and from your observations and feelings you have made a decision about whether or not you want to work with them as their therapist or refer them to someone else. You are now ready to fill out the "Summary Sheet" you will use while giving the Feedback to the family.

Fill out the "Summary Sheet" in a thoughtful way, incorporating the most significant things you have learned about the family during the first two interviews; their inherited and present process, their problems and the ways they handle them, the stated or unstated contract you see operating between husband and wife, and the family's goals. Also write on the "Summary Sheet" your own feelings about the kind of contract you will have to make with the family in order to work effectively with them.

FAMILY SCULPTURE

Description of Exercise

Family Sculpture is the family's primarily nonverbal statement about themselves through action, posture, gesture, and facial expressions. Using their bodies as a sculptor uses clay, they show their relationships telescoped in space and time. Events or attitudes are seen and experienced simultaneously by all. In sculpture bodies speak more directly and powerfully than words. All members have an equal opportunity to act and feel with their bodies what it is like to live in their family.

The interviewer acts as director, facilitator, and in special cases as therapist, asking and helping members to place themselves physically in relationship to one another, as they view themselves at specific times: close or apart; big or small; above or below; stationary or in motion; looking at or away from each other; gesturing in a way that shows their attitudes and feelings toward each other. When all members have worked out their positions and stances so that there is a consensus of accuracy within the whole family, the result is a living tableau, or a series of tableaux, depicting a multidimensional, focused image of the family.

Uses of Sculpture for the Interviewer and the Family. Sculpture can be used in several ways. To gather generalized information about the positive and negative ways the family interacts. To help you and the family see the complexity of their interrelationships. To clarify a point of confusion for you: e.g., do the children want to separate mother and father, and for what reason; or do mother and father use the children as buffers so they will not have to be close to one another? To try to get at material you think the family may be hiding: e.g., you suspect Mother is an alcoholic, but no one in the family has directly talked about it — you hope someone might be able to let this fact out during the emotional heat of the sculpture. To make apparent a game you think the family is playing: e.g., a protection game — it will become clear that Father is trying to protect all members as he tries to put his arms around the whole family at once. Sometimes a member will spontaneously suggest, through action, that the family has power to change their ways of interrelating. In one of our families the mother had her hands full of two small children. One began to cry. The father, who had never had much part in the child-rearing process, gently picked up the crying child, who let go of the mother's hand. The mother was able to reach that hand out to the father, and the whole family became closer.

Directing Family Sculpture

There are many ways of directing a sculpture. Workshops in sculpture techniques are given periodically by the Boston Family Institute, the Ackerman Center (New York), and others. What we offer here is a detailed account of the approach we used, basically a nonverbal equivalent of the History Taking, starting with the parents and adding each child in sequence.

Give the families a brief explanation of what you mean by Family Sculpture. Tell them why you are asking them to participate — "to give us all a clearer notion of how the family got to be the way it is." After asking the parents to stand up, say, "All of you are going to have a chance to be in the sculpture, but we're going to start with your parents, because they're the ones who started this family. I'd like the two of you [parents] to show us what your relationship was like at the point when you decided to get married." You may have to do some demonstrating here. "Did you feel close together?" Hug one of them or your co-interviewer if you have one. "Did you feel far apart?" Push them away and turn your back. "Did one of you feel dependent on the other?" Lean on someone. "I'd like you to express just how you felt about each other, using your bodies and actions, and without talking if possible."

Because most people are so used to talking, we found that we had to remind them quite frequently not to. Occasionally, however, a word or phrase will come out which is central to the family's system. Such a word or phrase can become very powerful when the speaker keeps repeating it — for example, when a suicidal person says, "I wish I were dead."

Most couples understand how to cooperate with these directions, some more imaginatively than others. Give them a chance to find their space — each may have quite a different notion of what it felt like then. They may both get into an embrace and then find that too hot, back away, find a more comfortable way of relating. One may feel close, the other not so close. They may line up like sparring partners, angry at "having" to get married. Allow whatever happens to happen. When they stabilize their position check it out with them: "Does that feel accurate — the way you felt about each other then and until your first child was born?"

Allow time for any adjustment of position; then call the oldest child by name: "Jimmy, here are your mother and father. Let's see what happens when you are born into this family." Jimmy will probably get into his mother's arms or directly between the two parents. Wherever and however he places himself, check out the accuracy of his placement with everyone. Then check out whether his being in the family now changes the relationship between father and mother. Can they still hug each other if that's what they were doing? Can they still be as close if Jimmy is between them? Can Mother contact Father if both her arms are around Baby Jimmy? Many couples demonstrated no major change after the first child. "He made us feel even closer," is a typical comment, or, "We can all still make contact with each other."

At this point note if the family seems to be easy and relaxed about physically contacting each other, or if they are having difficulty. If they are having trouble physically maintaining their positions, you may say, "I notice you're having a hard time staying in that position. Does it seem uncomfortable to you?" Help them find out where the discomfort is, what is causing it, and whether or not it represents some real Family Dynamic pain, e.g., the husband may sculpt himself in the position of supporting his wife. As she hangs on his neck, he begins to hurt physically — he develops a pain in the neck. Always check positions for the possible implications of sculpture pain. Is he in a position of power? Is the wife really pulling on him in a psychological sense? As the sculpture continues in time, see whether anything happens to change or relieve the sculpture pain. As children arrive, does the husband stop holding up his wife, relinquishing the power position? Or does he retain his painful power position — holding her up, and the children, too? Check here to see, as he holds up more and more people, if his neck is a painful spot for him in real life. If so, his neck pain may be a chronic physical ailment originating from a dysfunctional Family Dynamic.

Add each subsequent child to the sculpture. With each addition check out the accuracy of everyone's position, how each person feels about changes as they occur. Watch for physical comfort and discomfort always. Watch, especially in a large family, for parents' hands (usually the mother's) getting full of children, and for older children being pushed out of position by younger ones. Who can get close to, and touch, whom; who is untouchable? Who takes the power position? Who is isolated, and who is smothered ("we're such a close family")? Do the parents get pushed apart as children arrive, or are they able to maintain a strong relationship together even if only by eye contact? Point out to the family all the things you notice as they occur.

Finally, when all members have been added to the sculpture and have found their positions and gestures, ask the family, "Is that how it is in the family now?" Give them a chance to rearrange their positions if they feel it is necessary, and give them a chance to comment on the final sculpture, or on any part of the sculpture that they would like to talk about, using page 110 as a guideline.

Small Children. Although small children generally respond well to doing sculpture, as it involves less talking than most of the other exercises and more moving around, sometimes they become upset because something is happening which frightens them, or makes them sad or angry. We have found it best to help the child to say his/her feelings, and ask the child to try to wait and see what happens next. If the child is feeling left out because his/her turn has not come yet to be born, help the child to say that, and assure him/her that it will happen very soon. Sometimes children take this occasion when their parents are busy with their own feelings to act up when the parents have otherwise had them under tight control. What the parents do then will tell you something about the way the parents handle "outbreaks" — who does it and how — and what they consider an "outbreak."

Special Families

Families Who Are Rigid. Some families act immobile. Try as they might, they can neither invent positions for themselves nor hold those you may suggest for them. This may point to a deep-rooted problem — real immobilization in real life. Or it may point only to the fact that the family cannot conceptualize easily on a physical level, just as others have a hard time putting thoughts and feelings into words. You will have to ask such a family why they think they are immobilized during the sculpture, then use your own judgment about whether or not it is beneficial to continue the sculpture. Don't push.

Families Who Pretend. Pretending in Family Sculpture is a way of appearing to cooperate while denying feelings. We think families pretend when they are afraid to look at their feelings. For example, one of our families cooperated entirely with our sculpture directions, but when it came time to include the last child, who had died as a baby, the family did not make space for him in the sculpture. They "pretended" the child never existed. You can handle such families by accepting their view of events and simply proceed with the sculpture. Or you can point out that you think the family is not wanting to get into feelings for some reason or another. In any event, you are up against a form of solid family defense or boundary.

Families Who Say "No." You may have a family that refuses to participate. When this happened to us, it took us almost twenty minutes to believe what was happening. Mother vacillated, children fought with each other, Father flatly refused, Mother objected to Father's refusal, the children took sides, Father tried, Mother refused, and so on. We aren't certain what exactly we learned from this; we think that somewhere between Mother vacillating (as a signal to Father to refuse) and Father refusing (as a signal to Mother to vacillate) lies the answer. There was surely collusion on the part of everyone in the family not to let the sculpture happen.

How to Process the Sculpture for the Family

After all members are included, you can help the family process their sculpture. Since this is part of an evaluation, keep the processing low-keyed; that is, comment specifically on what you see without raising deep questions or making deep interpretations. When the contract we have with the families we interview is simply to observe, not to intervene or effect change, we try mainly to sum up what we see happening: "In a sculpture with seven people it's hard for everyone to have contact with one another," or, "Gerry, the motion you made with your arms looked like flying. We also noticed that though your body was facing away from the family, you looked back constantly at your parents."

Another way we helped families process the sculpture was to ask members to step out of the sculpture one by one, while one of us stood in for them, to check out how it looked to them. We asked: "Does the sculpture look accurate — is that the way you see people relating to each other?" With families we have seen in therapy we have gone on to ask, "What does it feel like to look at that sculpture of your family — to see yourself there?" And further, "Is there anything you would like to change about your position in the sculpture? What ways can you think of to change it? Move the people around the way you would like them to be."

A rule to remember while directing or processing the sculpture is not to make assumptions about the family or individuals in the family. Check out everything with them, and don't argue with their interpretations. You can point out that the father (for instance) looks uncomfortable twisted in a certain position, that you notice he's groaning, but if he says he's not uncomfortable, then abide by what he says he's feeling.

Many good things can happen for the family during a sculpture — confirmations of love, remembrances of times when they felt close and happy. When you see these, comment on them. Families need to hear their positive feelings about each other affirmed as often as possible, so they know what to build on.

When to Become "Therapist." We reiterate a strong warning here not to deliberately do sculpture as therapy unless trained to do so — that is, until you have done extensive work on yourself, have had supervised clinical training, and have participated in experiential sculpture workshops. There are times, however, when it will be appropriate for you to step out of the observer's role and into the therapist's, even if you haven't had all the necessary training. Sometimes a sculpture raises material for a whole family that needs to be dealt with on the spot so that the family is not left with a new unresolved problem. Sometimes stored body memories of fear, loneliness, anger, or loss will surface as members use their bodies to describe their interrelationships across time and space, and it will be important for you to help them deal with these feelings as openly as they can.

ASSESSING FAMILY SCULPTURE

Since you will be doing the sculpture as the final exercise, you will already know a great deal about the family and can have in mind, before you begin, some specific Skills, Negative Mechanisms, and Family Dynamics you want to clarify for yourself and for the family. If the family's *ability to get what you want* is low, for example, you can watch for difficulties members may have in physically contacting one another or in finding a comfortable position. If *accepting individual differences* is low, you can observe whether the whole family sculpts itself as a tight group, whether any members seem physically to want to break away. In a family that has trouble *risk taking*, you can look for closed stances — arms crossed across chests or stomachs, unable to reach out.

Families that use a lot of *joking, denying,* or *evading* in order to avoid facing their feelings about issues will use these same Negative Mechanisms in the sculpture — will either avoid getting into meaningful positions together, or will discount the idea that the sculpture has any relevance to real life — it's only a game, ha-ha. The *distracter* or *placater* in the family will have a terrific opportunity to act out during the sculpture. *Double messages* may be delivered with startling accuracy — literally on the one hand — and on the other hand. *Power* positions may become very clear — be ready to provide a chair for the power person to stand on "above" the others. A family that has difficulties maintaining privacy *boundaries* will demonstrate this in a physical way — members will be unable to get away from one another. If there is a *family lineup,* you can bet that it will appear. A family that has warm, good feelings about each other will show it in their bodies, in their facial expressions, in the way they contact each other. You will feel the warmth.

GIVING FEEDBACK TO THE FAMILY

The Feedback might start to flow quite naturally as a consequence of the Family Sculpture, as you or the family bring up questions about the way they interact. In such a case you will be able to use examples from the sculpture you have all just experienced to make the Feedback more meaningful.

Whether or not you decide to use the sculpture as an integral part of the Feedback, tell the family in as positive a way as possible what you have observed to be their process and the possible source of their difficulties. Discuss very broadly the Skills they do very well and those that need work. We feel people need to hear positive things before they can really take in negative things, and the negative things you say will have to be stated very carefully. Remember, the family knows very well that they have problems or they wouldn't have consulted you. Dwelling on negatives is not only unhelpful, it is also unnecessary. This is not to say that you cannot be honest with families. We tend to include our own personal experiences as anecdotes during negative parts of the Feedback — not emphasizing our triumphs, but rather our own foibles. It takes the heat off and reduces the bad news to a common experience. You can say honest things about areas in which a family needs to work in a way that assures them that there is hope, even sometimes humor, to be found in their plight.

We did not share scores with families. Somehow that smacks

of IQ numbers, school grades, tracking techniques that fix people in positions from which they feel they cannot move. To learn that they are "below average" on even one Skills score may be devastating to a family who have had the typical American educational experience — which means most of us.

It seems to be far more helpful to talk of comparisons only within the family's own Skills. For example, you might say, "Your family was so fantastic at negotiating that it seems as if it won't be too much of a job for us to get some other Skills working better. It looks as if you've inherited some old habits from your own families which aren't working very well for you now. I think there's a lot of work to do around being able to ask each other directly for what you want, which you parents never learned to do as children, and so haven't been able to teach these children. And some work on being able to see each other more clearly as individuals."

We went through the Skills for the families one by one, talking about them in practical ways, rather than using jargon. They accepted the information presented in this way, discussing the Feedback with us, and telling us of ways they thought they might make use of it.

MAKING A CONTRACT TO WORK WITH THE FAMILY

After you have finished the Feedback, give the family a chance to integrate what you have said. Get up and let everyone stretch, walk around for a few minutes. It's a lot of information, and the tension level may be very high no matter how carefully you have designed the session.

After everyone has settled back down again, tell them that you would like to work with them and why. Share your feelings about them as a family and as people. Explain your terms. Different family therapists have different ways of working — rules about the number of members who have to come to every session, the number of times they have to come, the limit on the number of times they may come, rules about lateness, phone calls, carrying out assignments. There is no right way to work, but you need to make clear what your rules are. Explain the reason for wanting to work with them as a family, rather than working with only the "problem person." Tell them that in order to work successfully you will need to make a contract with all of them.

Some families won't want to work with you, for whatever reason. Some will be open about their objections; others will equivocate, tell you that after all you have said to them they still think that "Johnny is the problem" and they don't want to be in family therapy. You will have to accept the fact that some people are not willing to explore ways of changing and would rather keep their problems invested in one person than change their system or themselves.

If the family wants to work with you, the real part of the contract will be that you all agree to work seriously, to be truthful, open, committed to yourselves as people, and committed to grow together.

REFERRING THE FAMILY

If you have decided for one reason or another that you cannot work with a family that wants to be in therapy, you will need to refer them to someone else. If your reason is a hang-up of your own, admit this in a noninjurious way, as openly as you can, so the family doesn't feel it's their fault. For example: "I am still working on my own feelings of anger at my father's drinking, and feel I wouldn't be able to be very objective as a therapist in this family, since some of you are angry at your father for drinking." If you can't work with the family because you don't have the skills to deal with the problems you feel it has, tell them honestly that you don't have the specific skills to help, but you feel confident that the people at XYZ Clinic do. Share with them the facts that you don't have the same kind of training or background, that you know you would not be as helpful to them as you would like to be. Help them understand that it is not because they are so sick, but that you are so untrained, which will be the plain truth. Don't make it heavy. Congratulate them for their commitment to learning and growing, and help them get started elsewhere. You might offer to share the evaluation you have just done with the XYZ Clinic, assuring the family they have not been wasting their time or yours — they have already learned something, and you have learned from them. It will have taken courage and commitment for the family to have come at all. However low their scores, remember it may be that very courage and commitment which can make growth possible with better trained therapists. Validate everything positive that you can.

Shopping

We feel it is crucial never to refer anyone to others unless you know those others very well. Clinics and psychiatrists should be willing to talk to you about their policies, philosophies, and methods of therapy in a way you understand, that allows you to ask questions. If they don't, go elsewhere. Remember that while you may not have a M.D., you do have the intelligence and common sense to decide what kind of people you trust. And it would be irresponsible for you not to use that common sense and intelligence. Check around with friends, do some shopping. Don't believe that certificates of any kind are guarantees of good therapy.

Chapter 10
Other Uses for the Exercises

Although we have presented the exercises as a sequential series for the purpose of evaluating families, all can be used in other ways. They can be used together or separately for a family already in therapy, as teaching aids for students in various professions wanting to learn about family process, and as learning experiences for members of a therapeutic group. They can also be used for crisis prevention and as a learning experience in your own family. We'll describe some of the ways we've used the exercises, and hope it may encourage you to adapt any of them to your own needs.

IN FAMILY THERAPY

History Taking

We have found it useful, with families we see, to fill out the History Taking forms over a period of time as we gather information. As we may never have a formal History Taking session with a family, we then have the information organized in a way that makes sense to us — helping us define what is old process, how the family sees themselves, and how they handle current issues.

In some families, it is evident that little information of any kind is shared between members. Here, it is useful when doing a History Taking, or partial History Taking, to do a great deal of checking-out between the members. Do they hear the information? Is it OK to hear the information? Is it OK to ask each other for information? Essentially, we try to open up the families in a non-threatening way, giving them permission to share facts and feelings with each other during therapy sessions. We then instruct them to try out the same kinds of sharing together at home so they can begin to make real changes in their communication patterns.

The History Taking technique can also be useful in dealing with a specific problem in a family, or with an individual. For instance, a History Taking was arranged for a twelve-year-old, whose parents had divorced when he was eight. Since that time, the parents and child had never talked all together, so that any problems having to do with their current complication relationships were never resolved. The parents were hostile toward each other and were afraid of getting into a bad argument in front of the child. Both parents agreed to come together and talk with the child, in therapy, about his past — his birth and early years. Aside from the obvious value for the child of hearing the facts about himself, this session demonstrated that fears of an argument were not justified. In fact, as long as they kept their discussion focused on the needs of the child, they were able to be quite comfortable with one another. This paved the way for future joint conversations outside therapy about issues like vacations, school problems, weekend visits, and so on, which was a great relief to all.

Draw a House

We have used the house exercise with a family who we felt gained more from nonverbal work than from verbal. The father had had very little education and found it difficult to talk to others in the family or to us. The mother was adept verbally and did most of the talking when she could get away with it. During the house exercise, the mother and children painstakingly replicated their own small suburban house down to the last doorknob. The father, however, filled in the background with snow-capped mountains and birds flying all around. There had been an issue of anger at the father who had often taken down his hunting rifle at the last minute and gone off in the woods alone or driven up to New Hampshire, where he camped out, fing and hunting. The rest of the family felt abandoned and the father felt contrite but would say very little except that he would try not to go off so much. After the picture was completed, we commented on the mountains.

The other family members scoffed, saying you couldn't see mountains from their house. He replied that he could see them — he knew just where they were. He began to tell us what it was like for him up there — how it was like being in a small patch of woods he had played in as a little boy, where he had felt safe from his two big brothers and where he had spent his happiest days. As he talked, it became clear to the rest that he did not go off to abandon them, but to regain some of the good feelings he needed when the pressures of a double job and a large family became too great. We then had the family negotiate about the part which most upset them — that he went off at the last minute and would not say why.

Role Card Game

A family complaining that nothing gets done around the house, or that one person is "doing it all," can benefit from the Role Card Game. This exercise demonstrates graphically the number of jobs there are, and who in fact does them. It then gives the therapist and the family an opportunity to look at possibilities of sharing responsibilities in a new, nonsexist way. It is interesting for the family to find out just how much they have automatically thought certain jobs belong to certain people — boys take out trash, for instance, and girls do dishes. In helping a family with the problem of job sharing we have found jobs are easier to exchange when using the cards than when just talking about the real jobs. Also, this exercise forces people to think about their jobs more clearly. For example, women frequently will not complain about a job they may greatly resent like grocery shopping, because it would be "stupid" to complain. Since, in the game, complaining is permitted while discarding, the feelings of resentment will come out. All kinds of hidden attitudes about jobs come out using cards — positive and negative. One father we know, who only cooked on the barbecue on Sundays in the summer, really liked to ccok. He opted to cook all the weekend meals instead of doing the "masculine" jobs he had done on weekends, when he saw that the mother and the oldest daughter preferred to do them. Making contracts around job sharing is part of family therapy. We have felt the cards help, especially if you ask the family to add other cards to include everything each one of them does.

The nonjob cards, or interaction cards, also provide insight to the family about the ways they relate to each other. We suggest that once family members get in touch with the implications of the roles they choose for themselves, or the ones which others tell them are true, that you can use in therapy the really wonderful exercises Virginia Satir has invented in *Peoplemaking*. Her exercises help people work out of those roles if they decide to discard them. Or if they have chosen negative roles, such as Placater, which they don't discard, the exercises can point out the pain involved in those roles, and open up the question of change.

When you are working with a family, use whatever roles are relevant for them, making changes and substitutions in our list as they occur to you.

Family Problems

This exercise can be a good tool for pointing out discrepancies in what members think the biggest problem is, and also for opening up any taboos about admitting or discussing problems. We seem to spend a lot of time in therapy pointing out that it's O.K. to have problems, and that everyone's problems are real for him/her. If a parent can listen to a child's problem, if a child can accept that a parent has problems, we find the family anxiety level drops. Problems then cease to be overwhelming and can be dealt with in a realistic way, and eventually resolved. Some problems, such as sudden job loss or serious physical illness are complex and not easily resolved. Even in these cases, however, the family's ability to deal with the emotional impact — the anger, fear, sadness — clears the way toward dealing with the logistics and effecting the compromises that must be made by all.

Asking for What You Want

We have used this exercise without the cards in subgroups in families. We ask members to hold each others' hands, look at each other, and ask directly for what they want most from that person. This can be terrifying for people who have never been able to ask directly for anything — even holding hands can be terrifying — and we are always supportive to all members. We might actively help a child ask for what he wants from Father, actively help Father say whether or not he can give it, and then help them both negotiate and make compromises when necessary. We point out where the two are communicating well and where they have difficulty communicating. We insist that the Asking exercise be a direct, two-person process. If Mother or Little Sister intervenes, we point out that Father and Son need to work this out between the two of them, but the others can be helpful by later commenting on what they see going on, and by offering, or demonstrating, suggestions to make the process work better. Again, this exercise opens up communication and helps give all members new Skills — the Skill to ask, the Skill to hear and respond honestly, the Skill to negotiate if need be. In therapy sessions with an eight-member family, we used the exercise, in one form or another, in almost every session.

Family Bonanza

Family Bonanza has been especially helpful to us in trying to help a family understand their negotiating, communicating, problem-solving, and decision-making patterns. In real-life problem solving, there are usually hidden old arguments, so that thrashing out how the family's real income should be spent, for example, is hard work. Emotions can be at such a high pitch that when the therapist intervenes, pointing out communication problems, it is very difficult for the family to hear. In a fantasy situation, without a heavy involvement in the subject matter, the usual patterns will still emerge, but will be easier to deal with. We have found it most helpful to tape the exercise, and then replay the tape, talking about what we hear happening, and asking the family to do the same. The learning from this can then be used effectively to negotiate their real issues.

Family Sculpture

We sometimes use the sculpture as we described it in Chapter 9. At other times we use the general technique with subgroups or even individuals to clarify feelings about a specific issue, or to help people get their feelings out into the open where they can be dealt with. For instance: a mother drags the whole family into therapy bristling with anger at her teenaged son who "won't listen" to her when she asks him to do things around the house. The rest of the family is there, she tells us, to confirm this — Johnny is a "rotten, no-good, kid". We know from her history that as a child she was forced into household drudgery and no one ever listened to her needs. We also know that she has never been able to acknowledge her own feelings of anger about the past. The first issue, therefore, is her unresolved feelings of anger and rejection, and not Johnny's behavior.

We asked each member of the family to turn his/her back on her when she asked any of them for something during the therapy session. We also turned our backs, re-creating in sculptural terms what her life had been like in the past, and how it felt in the present. She could no longer pin all that anger onto the son — all of us had behaved in the same way. None of us would listen to her. Even the therapists "didn't care," she said.

She began to cry, and then could tell her family how rejected and hurt she had felt when she was little, and how angry she was at the past. We helped her to say that she needed to be listened to and cared about. With her anger relegated to the past, the family could respond with caring instead of fear and resentment. The sculpture did not resolve the issues of rejection and anger on the spot. Rather, it removed the anger to the past, where she could later deal with it more appropriately, and forced the feeling of rejection into the open, giving us and the family a new handle on the problem of the "rotten kid." The mother, further, was able to see that she had confused her feelings about herself and her attitude toward her son, and to learn that in the present, whenever she felt those feelings toward him, she was usually reacting to the past. As her behavior changed, so did his.

IN GROUP THERAPY

All the exercises are adaptable for use in group therapy. The two we use most are the History and Family Sculpture.

A group leader might do a detailed History Taking with one member, having everyone in the group deal afterward with the feelings the History Taking brings up for that person and for h/self. The leader might then ask members to take each other's histories as a way of bringing out feelings from the past, and feelings of what it's like to interview and to be interviewed.

Basically, History Taking plunges group members into an awareness of how old family process has contributed to current family process and feelings about one's self. This exercise establishes a kind of common language and pool of information, helpful in dealing with all members' problems as the group continues. History Taking also sheds light on the group process — communication problems, anger, how relationships are formed. Of course, since people often relate to others in groups as substitutes for significant family members, it is essential to understand the original family relationships. Unless members also see the leader in therapy privately, it is otherwise difficult to have a clear idea of each person's history.

Sculpture techniques can be used to point up group process by sculpting a group relationship. Also, family-relationship issues can be sculpted in group. As director of a member's sculpture, the leader has that member ask others to be his/her family. An additional bonus here is that the actors often have strong feelings during their role play — even if the role is minor. The feelings of both the central person and the actors can reveal issues to be worked on in the group. For instance, during one such sculpture, a woman who was convincingly acting as someone else's bitchy, demanding stepmother had provided the central person with very valuable insights into the anger he had at that stepmother. Since our actress, however, was the soul of good manners and soft speech, she was horrified at her role behavior. Later in group she began to work on her feelings about her own bitchiness, about which she was ashamed; she had covered it up all of her life, using enormous amounts of energy to superimpose a mask of gentility. She was able to come to terms with anger as a real and valuable part of herself and to finally drop her mask. We felt that the acting part had enabled her to act herself while being someone else, whereas in real life she always acted like someone else to cover up her real self.

IN CRISIS PREVENTION

One of our original ideas for using this evaluation system was as a crisis prevention tool in a community health center — on the well-baby clinic model; that is, as a well-family checkup system. As major changes approach in the lives of families, such as the birth of children or grandchildren, children leaving home for school, divorce or remarriage of parents, marriage of younger members, moving, job change or loss, physical illness, or death, families could come into the clinic to evaluate their skills, and to work with a therapist in areas that are troublesome. We would hope that this kind of evaluation and follow-up, done routinely, would prevent crises from occurring.

IN YOUR OWN FAMILY

The best way to use these exercises for your own family is to persuade a friend to run them for you. The whole family can then listen to the tapes and do the evaluating together. If family members get into using the evaluating sessions to blame others, you'll have to give it up and ask your friend to do the evaluating. Be sure to be honest about your own part. If you have read the book, you may be tempted to change your own behavior to look good during the interviews. Unless you intend to change your behavior permanently, you will skew the analysis of your family system.

IN TRAINING COURSES

More and more people in the helping professions — teachers, school counselors, medical people, lawyers, probation officers, pastoral counselors, social workers, psychologists, psychiatrists — are wanting to learn about family process and therapy in order to better understand and deal with their clients. We feel that this book, including the Bibliography, can be used as a text for teaching family process, or that any of the exercises can be used separately for demonstrating family issues. A training group might use situations from their own families of origin to demonstrate problems families have, and then apply the exercises, using group members as stand-ins for family members. (We have found it best not to use current family problems as demonstration material, unless the group is specifically set up to do therapy for the person involved.)

Another technique would be for the training group to form one or more mock families. A mock family doing the House Drawing, for example, might get real insights into how hard it is to cooperate on a project, communicate without words, and define individual spaces — and can then discuss what might make these things easier for all. A mock family doing Family Bonanza would find out about each others' individual differences and value systems, and how these affect their negotiating together and ability to get what they want. The training group leader can keep all issues focused on the task at hand — to learn about family Skills, and what factors help or impede these Skills. Any of the exercises may be adapted to the individual needs of the class. A divorce lawyer will need to learn some specific techniques that may differ from those of a high school teacher or a practical nurse.

Appendix 1

Scoring and Numbers

How to Score Skills

In our original project with seven families, on which this evaluation technique is based, we tried to find a way to "grade" families that would be as nonjudgmental as possible. Obviously, there is no way to avoid the observer-view from coloring the scores since we come as observers with a set of values either subconsciously ingrained or deliberately arrived at. The work of Ray Birdwhistell, among others, points to the difficulties that nearly preclude monitoring objectively such a mass of data as we have collected, even if we were to attempt a statistical model.

Therefore, we have set out for you our own biases in Chapter 1. We have gone on to arrange a systematic scoring using 5 to 0 for the Skills of these families in as commonsense and objective a way as possible. You may have arguments with various of our original viewpoints. In those cases, you will be able to rethink whether our scores are consistent with your own values, or with those of your clients when you work with clients whose lifestyles are substantially different from your own. For example, it may be hard work with such a family to decide what is a putdown and what is a mere joke. You'll have to ask the family.

The Scale: 5 to 0. We felt that a scale of 5 to 0 was simpler and more appropriate than, say, a scale of 100 to 0, since the differences in family Skills would appear to be too precisely measured on a larger number scale. Within the range of 5 to 0, therefore, we suggest keeping to the closest multiple of .5 on each skill, using 0, 0.5, 1, 1.5, 2, 2.5, 3, 3.5, 4, 4.5, 5.

Converting All Numbers into 5 to 0. In Appendix 2, in the detailed scoring directions for each exercise, there are sections titled "Fill out Skills Sheet." After following the instructions for each Skill to either add, subtract, and/or divide, much of the time you will come out with a number (sometimes in decimal form) which will not directly correlate to our scale of 5 to 0. In order to have these numbers fit on a 5 to 0 scale we have given you a conversion formula for each of those Skills, always putting the final score first. There are, however, Skills which are figured by simply adding certain elements and dividing by the number of family members, and this number fits the scale directly. In order to have no confusion about which is which, we have also always given you a formula with those Skill-scoring directions.

To get a clear idea of what we mean, turn to the Role Card Game in Appendix 2. For "Step 4, Fill out Skills Sheet, *Shared Facts, Meanings, Values,*" the directions are "Add up the family's 'Wrongs' and 'Not Belongs.' Divide this number by the number of people in the family. . . . Score: 5=0; 4=2; 3=4; 2=6; 1=8; 0=10 or more." Turn to pages 142–145, where you will find the family's "Role Charts." If you will total the "Wrongs" and "Not Belongs," you will get the number 7. Dividing 7 by the number of people in the Smith family (4) gives you the number 1.7 (approximately). Looking at the conversion formula, you see that the closest number to 1.7 is 2, so that your raw score will convert to a final 4.

In the same exercises you will see *"Responsibility,"* with directions, page 140. Reading those, you will notice that although the raw score is merely an addition problem, it too requires a conversion formula as the numbers you will come up with are inversely related to our 5 to 0 scale.

In some exercises you will be asked to figure a percentage. There is a general formula for converting percentages: 5=100%, 4=80%, 3=60%, 2=40%, 1=20%, 0=0%. In order to avoid confusion, however, we have repeated that formula for conversion at the end of each of those Skills in which percentages are used. An example of this will be found on page 149, "Asking for What You Want, *Step 3,* Fill out Skills Sheet, *Straight Talking.*" The Smith family has a percentage of 88 in column 4 and 70 in column 5. Averaging these two numbers to 79, and converting, using the formula, they have a score of 4.

Inferential Numbers. In Draw a House and the Role Card Game, five of the scores for Skills are not based on hard data. The quality of the Skills must be inferred from the nonverbal clues, the kind of feeling in the family — is there a sense that the family is having fun, or is the House Drawing a grim chore? Are they getting any satisfaction out of the drawing — is the house itself what they all want, with room for compromise, or do they feel as if it is a failure, perhaps as they are failures at working together? Can members identify themselves within the family as individuals? Very often one of the parents is so busy during the exercise that he/she cannot find time to put anything personal into the drawing. Or one child will simply do what another does. It will help, when these directions to score "inferentially" come up, to turn to the definitions of the Skills involved and try to think of how you imagine a happy, healthy family doing the exercise and compare that to the family under observation. Better yet, find yourself a healthy family to practice with.

You will be looking for some sense of fun, for warmth and affection, when you ask the question, "Do you have any fun together at dinner and in the evening?" in the Role Card Game under *"Ability to Play."* Being careful to ask each person to listen to what all say, you will hear a consensus that dinner time is a good time for the family, or that it isn't, and why. You know what it's like at a happy family dinner table. People are relaxed and sharing. No one has done all of the work and is sitting there exhausted and angry, while the others gulp down their food, only to be off to the TV.

We've given you guidelines for questions to ask yourself on each of these Skills, but you will have to make your own judgments as you gain experiences of your own.

How to Score Negative Mechanisms

On page 176 is a filled-in "Negative Mechanisms Sheet." You will be keeping a frequency count rather than a score for all of the Negative Mechanisms in each of five exercises. This is a way for you to see how many times a family uses any Negative Mechanism, to help you in evaluating them. When we do therapy, we make note of these and point them out when they occur. "I notice that you interrupted John just now." We also have included a "Negative Mechanism Frequencies Table," based on our evaluations of seven families, so that you can get some notion of how often any one of them might occur.[1]

WHAT OUR SCORES MEAN

We found that our healthiest family ranged from 4.75 in *"Openness to the Outside"* to 2.5 in *"Responsibility."*[2] Their average, without weighting Skills at all, was 3.81. Our least healthy family ranged from 0.5 in *"Ability to Get"* and *"Decision Making"* to 2.5 on *"Responsibility,"* with an average of all Skills scores of 1.31. The implications of these scores based on our small sample are several. The first family was having some difficulties of which they were well aware (and subsequently did some work on). We could show them that where they scored low were trouble areas, and that where they scored high were strong points which they could put to use to resolve the struggle in the family. The unhealthy family was in such bad shape that they had already been referred by the school to the outpatient department of a psychiatric hospital. We saw them before they had begun work, and it was clear to us that only a team of very experienced professionals could have made any impact on them.

Table 2, "Skills Scores For Each Family," may be helpful to you in determining whatever you think is a "below working level" score.

[1] See Table 1, pages 182–183.
[2] See Table 2, page 184.

Numbers, You, and the Family

Fools rush in where angels fear to tread, and layfolk, or those untrained in family therapy, need to find for themselves some line across which they do not dare to tread. Looking at the seven-family average (2.84) score in the Skills scores table, you will have to make a judgment about whether a family is so unhealthy that it is necessary for you to refer them to professionals. Family E, with essentially the same average (2.85) as the family average of all seven families, would be difficult for a layperson. We cannot say what that score is for you. As beginners ourselves, we have our own lines somewhere around 2. A family which goes below 2 has too few abilities in general for us to work with and needs to be seen by a team of more experienced people. For us to try, we feel, would give the family another experience of themselves as failures as a family. It would also be discouraging for us. All of us have to work where we are most effective. Of course we hope that as we become more experienced, we can risk more. And as you become more experienced, you will be able to risk more. So, start off modestly, and see how it works.

Appendix 2

Scoring the Exercises

HISTORY TAKING

Step 1. Fill out the family's answers to all questions on the History Taking forms when you listen to the tape, unless you are able to fill them out while taking the family's history. Working together as co-interviewers, we alternated questioning and writing.

Step 2. Fill out Skills Sheet.

Although the History is not scored by numbers, as the other exercises are, you may want to write pertinent notes on the bottom of the Skills Sheet on the following Skills: *Straight Talking/ Responding; Shared Facts, Meanings, Values; Openness Intra Family; Responsibility; Positive Contact with Each Other; Ability to Get What You Want; Limit Setting; Internally Chosen Roles, Openness to the Outside.*

These notes can be brief. For example: "Family talks straight except father, who evades questions re childhood." "No member knows how to ask directly for what he/she wants."

Step 3. Fill out Family Dynamics/Nonverbal Sheet.
Make notes on *secrets, myths, taboos; anger; sex; death; misfortune."*

Step 4. Fill out Summary Sheet.
Write down what you think the marital partners' contract is with each other. See Smith Family Summary Sheet, page 180, for example.

Step 5. Fill out History Taking Analysis.
Fill in the name and date of birth of each family member.
For Husband and Wife:
Fill in *Family Background*, i.e., relevant information from the History Taking on their parents' and grandparents' class, religion, sex roles, family climate, decision making, emotional stability, family taboos, and attitudes toward sex, death, money.

Fill in *Personal History*, i.e., relevant information from the History Taking on their own upbringing — class, religion, number of siblings and birth order, family expectations, punishment, anger, caring, asking/getting, problems, illnesses, feelings about themselves as children and in the present.
For Children:
Fill in *Personal History*, i.e., relationships with siblings, parents, friends; family expectations, taboos, punishment, anger, caring, asking/getting, problems, illnesses, feelings about themselves.

DRAW A HOUSE

See filled-in "Smith" working sheets:
  Nonverbal and Limit Setting Sheet, page 135;
  Nonverbal Notes, page 136;
  Drawing Notes, pages 137, 138.

Step 1. Make a Nonverbal and Limit Setting Sheet.

Step 2. Transfer from Nonverbal Notes all p's (positive interactions), n's (negative interactions), tp's (positive touching), and tn's (negative touching) onto *Nonverbal Interaction Chart*.

Step 3. Fill out Drawing Notes by looking at the family's drawing: Space on Paper, Messages, Labels. Copy the family's drawing if you think it is helpful to you.

Step 4. Transfer *Takeovers* and *Distractions* from Drawing Notes and Nonverbal Notes onto *Limit Setting Chart* on Nonverbal and Limit Setting Sheet. Note any successful limit setting on the chart.

Step 5. Fill out Negative Mechanisms Sheet:
a. Total number of T's on *Limit Setting Chart* = *Speaking for Others*.
b. Total number of tn's from *Nonverbal Interaction Chart* = *Putdowns;* written *Messages* from Drawing Notes may be *Putdowns*.
c. Fill in other Negative Mechanisms such as *Distractions, Giving Orders, I Won't Play, Placating,* whether these are nonverbal or you hear them on the tape. As you listen to the tape, fill in verbal Negative Mechanisms: *Unnecessary Questions, Jokes, Putdowns* — whatever is relevant. Since this is essentially a nonverbal exercise, there may not be much information from the tape.
d. Make any necessary *Notes* on above Negative Mechanisms (who does what to whom) on the back of the Negative Mechanisms Sheet.

Step 6. Fill out Family Dynamics/Nonverbal Sheet:
a. Note any *assumption making* in answer to your questions "What house were you drawing?" and "Were there any surprises?"
b. Note any *sexism* from the Drawing Notes and from looking at the drawing.
c. Note the *power structure* (or lack of any power structure) by looking at the Drawing Notes (who takes charge of drawing and/or messages) and the *Nonverbal Interaction Chart* (who initiates and/or receives most interactions).
d. Note family and individual *boundaries* from looking at the drawing. Note if a member places h/self only outside the house.
e. Note any *family alliances* from the *Nonverbal Interaction Chart* (which shows who relates to whom in the family); also from looking at the drawing for a "lineup."
f. Fill in any additional *Nonverbal Notes*.

Step 7. Fill out Skills Sheet:
a. *Openness Intra Family:* The total number of tp's and tn's (page

135) divided by the number of people in the family.
SCORE: 5 = 5 (or more); 4 = 4; 3 = 3; 2 = 2; 1 = 1; 0 = 0.
b. *Positive Contact with Each Other:* The total number of p's and tp's (page 135) divided by the number of people in the family.
SCORE: 5= 20; 4 = 16; 3 = 12; 2 = 8; 1 = 4; 0 = 0.
c. *Ability to Play:* SCORE: 5 to 0 inferentially.
d. *Ability to Get What You Want:* Average scores for I and II below:
   i. Is house one, whole house with perspective?
      SCORE: 5 to 0 inferentially.
   ii. Does whole family work together (willingly cooperate) on drawing at least once?
      SCORE: 5 *or* 0.
e. *Accepting Individual Differences:* The percentage of members indicating selves clearly and appropriately on the drawing.
SCORE: 5 to 0 inferentially.
   5 = 100%; 4 = 80%; 3 = 60%; 2 = 40%; 1 = 20%; 0 = 0%.
f. *Limit Setting:* The total number of *Takeovers* plus *Distractions*, minus the number of successful *Limit Settings* (page 135).
SCORE: 5 = 0; 4 = 2; 3 = 4; 2 = 6; 1 = 8; 0 = 10.
g. *Openness to the Outside:* SCORE: 5 to 0 inferentially.

Appendix 2

Nonverbal and Limit Setting Sheet   Name: __SMITH__

Nonverbal Interaction Chart

Total Initiations	Initiator	Recipients			
		JOHN	MARY	BILLY	SUZY
p 16 tp 8	JOHN	/////	p 8 tp 8	p 4	p 4 tp 3
p 15 tp 2 n 1 tn 1	MARY	p 7	/////	p 4	p 4 tp 2 n 1 tn 1
p 8 n 1	BILLY	p 6	p 1	/////	p 1 n 1
p 7 tp 7	SUZY	p 2 tp 7	p 2	p 3	/////
	Subtotals:	p 15 tp 7	p 11 tp 8	p 11	p 9 tp 5 n 2 tn 1
	Totals:	22	19	11	17

Key: p = positive interaction (nontouching)
      n = negative interaction (nontouching)
      tp = positive touching
      tn = negative touching

Totals: p = **46**   tp = **20**
         n = **2**   tn = **1**

Limit Setting Chart

Initiators	Recipients				General T	Distraction
	JOHN	MARY	BILLY	SUZY		
JOHN	/////					
MARY	T T	/////		T		
BILLY			/////			
SUZY		T	T T	/////	T	XXXX XXX

Key: X = Distraction
      T = Takeover
      L = Appropriate Limit Setting on Takeover or Distraction

Nonverbal Notes (with comments added)　　　　　　SMITH

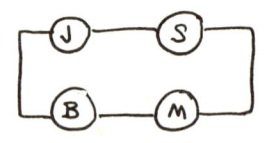

```
┌──(J)───(S)──┐
│             │
└──(B)───(M)──┘
```

J tp M　(John taps Mary on arm)
J p M　(John smiles at Mary)
M p J
J p S
J p B
B p J
S tp J
S p B
S distraction: calls dog to walk across paper, nobody sets a limit.
J tp S
M tn S　(Mary pushes Suzy out of the way)
B n S　(Billy sticks his tongue out at Suzy)

Family changes position:

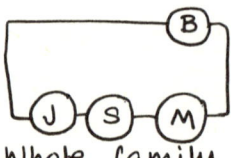

```
┌─────(B)─────┐
│             │
└─(J)─(S)─(M)─┘
```

Whole family works together
M p J
　　etc. . . .

Drawing Notes   Name: SMITH

Space on Paper: Complete, lively, lots of activity

Messages:
- M: "cabin"
- S: "mine's not"
- S: "House here"
- B: "I don't know"
- J: "blueprint plot plan"
- B: "What's that?"
- S: "If you don't like my pic. why don't you draw?"
- S: "Yecch"
- M: "Turn over the paper"

Labels: First names on all bedrooms
Names on rooms - kitchen, diningroom, livingroom, bathroom
Names on activity spaces - garden, pool, pottery room

(over)

Who Drew What in Sequence, with Takeovers

Take-overs	Who	What
Gen.T	S	outlines house
	M	"cabin"
	S	"mine's not"
		"House here"
	J	"blueprint plot plan"
	J	extends roof line
	B	"I don't know"
	M	kitchen addition
T	S	Front door - draws Mary
	B	own room with details
	J	basketball net on garage
	M	dogs outside house
	B	car - much detail
	S	own room - clothes on floor
	J	fireplace - draws self
T	M	mess in Suzy's room
	B	trunk in attic
T	S	Billy talking on phone
	B	"What's that?"

Take-overs	Who	What
	S	"If you don't like my pic. Why don't you draw?"
T	M	John's chicken coop
	J	garden
	B	Greek detail on roof
T	S	"Yeach" in Billy's corner
	M	Swimming pool with self
	J	bathroom - self in shower singing
	S	sun - clouds
	M	shrubs
	J	fireplace in own bedroom
	M	"turn over the paper"
	J	pottery room
T	M	John in garden
DIRECTION: "put selves on paper"
	B	in own room
	B	by basketball net
	S	in own room

ROLE CARD GAME

See filled-in "Smith" working sheets:
Role Charts, pages 142–145.

Step 1. Make a Role Chart for each family member. Put the member's name on the top and leave space for seven columns:
+ (for positive interaction roles)
− (for negative interaction roles)
Chosen (for roles the member chose for h/self)
Laid on (for all roles laid on the member by others, whether he/she accepted them or not)
Wrong (for roles laid on the member that he/she thinks are wrong and will not accept)
Not Belong (for roles others said were not accurate for the member whether the member had chosen them or others had laid them on)
Rejected (for roles the member discarded at the end of the game)

Step 2. Fill out a Role Chart for each family member. List their roles and fill in the appropriate columns for each. Be sure in the *Laid On* and *Not Belong* columns to write the names of the people who lay on the role or say it is inaccurate. You will get this information from both the role cards and papers the family has done up in elastics for you, and from listening to the tape for what the members have laid on, rejected, said were wrong for them, or did not belong to others. There will be some duplicating between the tape and the lists, but hang in there.

Step 3. Fill out Negative Mechanisms Sheet:
a. *Putdowns:*
    i. The number of negative roles laid on others.
    ii. The number of verbal putdowns you hear on the tape.
    iii. The number of positive roles in the *Not Belong* columns; e.g., Billy and Mary do a double putdown of Suzy, saying *Truthteller* does not belong to her.

b. *Self-Putdowns:* The number of negative roles the family chooses for self, e.g., Mary chooses *Blamer*. Also the number of incidental *Self-Putdowns* you hear on the tape.
c. While you're listening to the tape, fill in the number of *Unnecessary Questions, Inappropriate Jokes,* and any other Negative Mechanisms you hear.
d. Note on the back of the sheet specifics about who does which Negative Mechanisms.

Step 4. Fill out Skills Sheet:
a. *Shared Facts, Meanings, Values:* Add up the family's *Wrongs* and *Not Belongs*. Divide this number by the number of people in the family. (The Smiths have a score of 4, with very few *Wrongs* or *Not Belongs,* meaning little discrepancy between how members see themselves and how others in the family see them.)
   SCORE: 5 = 0; 4 = 2; 3 = 4; 2 = 6; 1 = 8; 0 = 10 or more.
b. *Responsibility:* Count 1 for each job never picked up by anyone in the family. Also count 1 for each job not shared by at least two members. Total the unpicked up and unshared jobs.
   SCORE: 5 = 0; 4 = 5; 3 = 10; 2 = 15; 1 = 20; 0 = 24.

Note: If it is not appropriate or relevant for a family to pick up a certain job, e.g., *Gives Small Kids Baths* in the Smith family, disregard the card in the scoring. Also, if a family has worked out a balanced system for house jobs that does not always include sharing each job, (an equal job splitting, for example, or a professional person to wash floors) disregard inappropriate cards in the scoring.

c. *Positive Contact with Each Other:* Total the + cards the members give each other. Divide the total by the number of people in the family.
   SCORE: 5 = 3; 4 = 2.5; 3 = 2; 2 = 1.5; 1 = 1; 0 = 0.
d. *Ability to Play:* From the answer to your question "Do you have fun at dinner and in the evenings?" you will infer the family's *Ability to Play.*
   SCORE: 5 to 0 inferentially.

e. *Accepting Individual Differences:* Divide the total number of rejects by the number of people in the family.
   SCORE: 5 = 5; 4 = 4; 3 = 3; 2 = 2; 1 = 1; 0 = 0. Is it possible for members to reject roles, change the system, be individual? Mary, e.g., is able to unload a lot of jobs, but Suzy is not able to reject *Blamer, Distracter* and *Victim.* John is not able to reject anything, and may be locking himself into playing family White Knight or perfect person.
f. *Internally Chosen Roles:* Total the family's positive interaction roles. Divide total by the number of people in the family.
   SCORE: 5 = 5; 4 = 4; 3 = 3; 2 = 2; 1 = 1; 0 = 0. Does the family as a whole see itself interacting positively?

Step 5. Fill out Family Dynamics/Nonverbal Sheet.

If you see any of the following Family Dynamics either in how the family interacts while playing the game or in your final adding up of the game's results, note specifics about what they are and who is involved in them: *sexism, scapegoating, power, family alliances, anger, emotional support, and hidden agenda.*

Fill out Nonverbal Notes, using page 82 as a guide.

When a Family Needs Therapy 142

Role Chart   Name: JOHN SMITH

Role	+	−	Chosen	Laid on	Wrong	Not Belong	Rej.
Disciplinarian			✓				
Fixer			✓				
Drink Maker				Mary			
Responsible for Everything			✓				
Outdoor Worker			✓				
Washes Dishes			✓				
Puts Kids to bed			✓				
Holiday Manager				Mary			
Table Clearer			✓				
Understanding One	+			Suzy Billy			
Truth teller	+		✓				
Creative One	+		✓				
Happy Person	+		✓				
Negotiator	+		✓				
Placater		−	✓				
Totals	5	1	12	4	0	0	0

Appendix 2

Role Chart   Name: **MARY SMITH**

Role	+	−	Chosen	Laid on	Wrong	Not Belong	Rej.
Washes Dishes			✓				✓
Floorwasher			✓				✓
Cook			✓				
Puts Kids to bed			✓				
Household Organizer			✓				
Holiday Manager			✓				
Cleans up after Snacks			✓				✓
After-meal Kitchen Cleanup			✓				✓
Big Filthy Jobs			✓				✓
Unloads Dishwasher			✓				✓
Food Shopper			✓				
Meal Planner			✓				
Errand Runner			✓				
Rule Maker			✓				
Responsible for Everything			✓				
Blamer		−	✓				✓
Truthteller	+		✓				
Creative One	+			John Billy			
Helpful One	+			Billy			
Totals	3	1	17	3	0	0	7

Role Chart   Name: BILLY SMITH

Role	+	−	Chosen	Laid on	Wrong	Not Belong	Rej.
Tablesetter			✓				
Washes Dishes			✓				
Outdoor Worker			✓				
Table Clearer			✓				
Trash Person			✓				
Pet Feeder			✓				✓
Helpful One	+		✓				
Truthteller	+		✓				
Lone Wolf		−	✓	Suzy		John Mary	
Understanding One	+			Mary			
Distracter		−		Suzy			
Creative One	+			John	✓		
Totals	4	2	9	4	1	2	1

Appendix 2

Role Chart   Name: SUZY SMITH

Role	+	−	Chosen	Laid on	Wrong	Not Belong	Rej.
Washes Dishes			✓				✓
Pet Feeder			✓				✓
Table Setter			✓				✓
Table Clearer			✓				
Creative One	+		✓				
Truthteller	+		✓			Billy Mary	
Blamer		−		Billy			
Helpful One	+			John			
Distracter		−		Mary	✓		
Happy Person	+			John			
Victim		−	✓			John	
Totals	4	3	7	4	1	3	3

FAMILY PROBLEMS

See filled-in "Smith" working sheet:
Problem Chart, page 148; Special Notes to Reader on Filling out the Problem Chart, page 147.

Step 1. Make a Problem Chart.

Step 2. On the Problem Chart, under *Content of Cards,* write the individuals' problems, just as they wrote them, so you will have the problems for reference.

Step 3. Fill out the Problem Chart as you listen to the tape.

Use the key on the chart (R = Risk Taking, etc.). The "Special Notes to Reader on Filling out the Problem Chart" on page 147 shows our process in filling out the chart. The discussion on "Assessing Family Problems," pages 84–87, is also a guide. The filled-out Problem Chart and the tape will contain all the information you need to fill out the Skills Sheet and Negative Mechanisms Sheet.

Step 4. Fill out Skills Sheet.
a. *Risk Taking:* Percentage of members with R's on Problem Chart
b. *Openness Intra Family:* Percentage of members with F's on Problem Chart.
c. *Openness to the Outside:* Percentage of members with O's on Problem Chart.

SCORE (each): 5 = 100%; 4 = 80%; 3 = 60%; 2 = 40%; 1 = 20%; 0 = 0%.

Step 5. Fill out Negative Mechanisms Sheet.

Take from the Problem Chart the number of *Evasions, Denials, Double Messages, Speaking for Others, Blaming, Inappropriate Jokes, Placating, Putdowns, Self-Putdowns.* Also add any other Negative Mechanisms you have heard on the tape.

Step 6. Fill out Family Dynamics/Nonverbal Sheet.

Make specific notes, naming names of members involved in any of the following Family Dynamics that you notice, either while the family is doing the exercise or afterward while you are listening to the tape: *collusions; secrets, myths, taboos; hidden agenda, assumption making; scapegoating;* dealing with *death;* and *anger.* Use the discussion on pages 86–87 as a guide.

Fill out *Nonverbal Notes,* using page 87 as a guide.

Special Notes to Reader on Filling out the Problem Chart

Some of the sequence of the Family Problems discussion as noted on this chart is: John says, "I can't maintain myself very well as an individual in the family." He wrote a serious problem on the card (*O*), and stated it in a way that directly involved family feelings (*R*). In response Mary said, "I always thought that was the trouble around here; we are *too* individualistic! [laughs]." She gets a *J*. Billy responds, "Mom, let's hear what Dad means." He gets an *F* for saying a forward-moving sentence. This sequence is then stopped by Suzy, who interrupts with "I want to go next!" (*I*). All glare at her.

Mary speaks: "I find the biggest problem is that I can't get along with Suzy, who is going through a teenage phase and she's just horrible to live with." Mary gets an *O* for writing her problem down, an *R* for stating a problem which certainly involves family feelings, and a *PD* for putting Suzy down in the process. Responses to Mary are: John placates (*P*), saying, "Now, now, you two, it's not *that* bad!"; Billy puts Suzy down too, (*PD*), saying, "It is too, Dad. Suzy is a pain!" Suzy interrupts again (*I*), "I want to go next." All glare at her.

Billy speaks: "The biggest problem is Mom and Dad have trouble with Suzy." He gets an *O*, and an *R* and an *X* for *Speaking for Others,* since it's their problem. John evades neatly with "I don't know what you mean," and Suzy says "Yeah, *you* never have any trouble, you're such a momma's boy" (*PD*). Mary says nothing (*E*).

When a Family Needs Therapy 148

Problem Chart   Name: **SMITH**

	Speakers			
Responders	JOHN	MARY	BILLY	SUZY
JOHN	O R	P	E	P
MARY	J	OR PD	E	B
BILLY	F	PD	OR X	F
SUZY	I	I	PD	O R

Key: R = Risk Taking   SPD = Self-Putdowns
      O = Openness to the Outside   J = Inappropriate Jokes
      F = Openness Intra Family   B = Blames
      E = Evasions   I = Interruptions
      P = Placating   X = Speaking for Others
      D = Denials   DM = Double Messages
     PD = Putdowns

Content of Cards:

JOHN: Maintaining myself as an individual
MARY: Not getting along with Suzy
BILLY: Mom and Dad have trouble with Suzy
SUZY: Not enough privileges

ASKING FOR WHAT YOU WANT

See filled-in "Smith" working sheets:
  Want Cards (side 1), page 152;
  Want Cards (side 2), page 153;
  Question Cards, page 154;
  Asking Chart, page 155.

Step 1. Make Asking Chart with the following Skills headings for each family member:
1. *Risk Taking:* Does person ask *directly* for something for h/self?
2. *Listening:* Does Col. 1 on Question Cards equal the verbal request from others (i.e., did members hear exactly what each person asked them for)?
3. *Ability to Get:* Does Col. 3 on Question Cards equal the verbal response from others (i.e., did members hear exactly others' responses to their requests)?
4. *Straight Talking:* Does verbal request equal a request written on Want Card?
5. *Straight Responding:* Does Col. 2 on Question Card equal a verbal response (i.e., are members clear about whether or not they can give others what they were asked for)?
6. *Positive Contact with Each Other:* Is verbal response affirmative?

Step 2. Fill out Asking Chart. Use information from the Want Cards and Question Cards which the family has filled out. For the verbal requests and responses listen to the tape. Use "yes," "no," or "1/2" in filling out the chart; "1/2" will stand for a "maybe" answer, or a qualified answer "yes, if . . ." or "no, unless . . ."; "1/2" will also stand for an answer that has affirmative wording but sounds uncommitted.

Step 3. Fill out Skills Sheet:
a. *Straight Talking/Responding:* Percentage of total "yeses" in Cols. 4 and 5 on Asking Chart.
  SCORE: $5 = 100\%$; $4 = 80\%$; $3 = 60\%$; $2 = 40\%$; $1 = 20\%$; $0 = 0\%$.

b. *Listening:* Percentage of total "yeses" in Col. 2 on Asking Chart.
SCORE: 5 = 100%; 4 = 80%; 3 = 60%; 2 = 40%; 1 = 20%; 0 = 0%.
c. *Risk Taking:* Percentage of total "yeses" in Col. 1 on Asking Chart.
SCORE: 5 = 100%; 4 = 80%; 3 = 60%; 2 = 40%; 1 = 20%; 0 = 0%.
d. *Positive Contact with Each Other:* Percentage of total "yeses" in Col. 6 on Asking Chart.
SCORE: 5 = 100%; 4 = 80%; 3 = 60%; 2 = 40%, 1 = 20%; 0 = 0%.
e. *Ability to Get What You Want:* Percentage of total "yeses" in Col. 3 on Asking Chart.
SCORE: 5 = 100%; 4 = 80%; 3 = 60%; 2 = 40%; 1 = 20%; 0 = 0%.

Step 4. Fill out Negative Mechanisms Sheet:
a. *Evasions:* Any nonresponse to a request. Any blanks on the Want Cards or Question Cards. Also any verbal or written "I don't know's," "maybe's," "not sure's," question marks, if these are patently avoiding a definite answer. (Sometimes these responses are appropriate, and you may have to make a judgment here about the context; e.g., "I don't know [what Mother asked me for], if the mother has been very unclear in her request.
b. *Putdowns:* Verbal, or on the cards.
c. *Denials:* Verbal, or on the cards.
d. *Other Negative Mechanisms:* Add whatever you hear on the tape.
e. Note on the back of the Negative Mechanisms Sheet specifics about who does what.

Step 5. Fill out Family Dynamics/Nonverbal Sheet:
a. *Hidden Agenda:* Note any members who have a hidden agenda and what you think the agenda is. (See our margin notes on the Question Cards sheet. On the tape John jokes in

response to Mary's request for "more time"; John's hidden agenda is his anger toward Mary for her behavior to Suzy. Also see our notes on Want Cards, side 1, where Mary's hidden agenda shows up on her written request, "love forever," which she changes to "more time" in the verbal asking.)
b. *Assumption Making:* Note who makes assumptions about whom. See our margin notes on Want Cards. Also the discussion of "Assumption Making," page 92.
c. *Anger; Emotional Support; Sex:* Make specific notes about what you hear and see, using page 93 as a guide.

Fill out *Nonverbal Notes,* using page 93 as a guide.

When a Family Needs Therapy

Want Cards (side 1)   Name: __SMITH__

Tape Content Where Different:

JOHN
I WANT FROM MARY: Sympathy to Suzy
I WANT FROM BILLY: More friendship
I WANT FROM SUZY: her to grow up happy

(HA) John's anger at Mary

MARY
I WANT FROM JOHN: love forever
I WANT FROM BILLY: to be able to show his anger to me and others
I WANT FROM SUZY: more help in house and patience when I ask for it.

(HA) "spend more time being close in future."

PD: "Grow up - stop being a pain - be helpful."

BILLY
I WANT FROM JOHN: companionship
I WANT FROM MARY: more distance
I WANT FROM SUZY: to realize my needs as well as hers

SUZY
I WANT FROM JOHN:
I WANT FROM MARY: not to say no so much
I WANT FROM BILLY: to use his Things, to stop teasing me

E: (says nothing)

Key: D = Denials   HA = Hidden Agenda
      E = Evasion   PD = Putdown

(over)

Want Cards (side 2)

JOHN	Assumptions
MARY WANTS FROM ME: faithfulness	
BILLY WANTS FROM ME: friendship	
SUZY WANTS FROM ME: fatherliness	(A) Suzy evades asking

MARY	
JOHN WANTS FROM ME: understanding for Suzy	
BILLY WANTS FROM ME: more support	(A) Billy wants more distance
SUZY WANTS FROM ME: patience	

BILLY	
JOHN WANTS FROM ME: he just wants me	(A) John wants more friendship
MARY WANTS FROM ME: to be good	(A) Mary wants him to show more anger
SUZY WANTS FROM ME: I don't know	E

SUZY	
JOHN WANTS FROM ME:	E
MARY WANTS FROM ME: not being such a procrastinator	
BILLY WANTS FROM ME: not to use his things	

Key: E = Evasion   A = Assumption Making

When a Family Needs Therapy 154

Question Cards　　　　　　　　　　　Name: SMITH

	Col. 1	Col. 2	Col. 3	Verbal Response Content Where Different from Col. 2:
JOHN	What Did Each Person Ask You For?	Do You Think You Can Give It to Them?	Do You Think You Can Get What You Asked for from Them?	
MARY	love	yes	yes	
BILLY	companionship	yes	yes	J,J: two jokes
SUZY	nothing, that I be as I am	yes	yes	E: (no response)
MARY	What Did Each Person Ask You For?	Do You Think You Can Give It to Them?	Do You Think You Can Get What You Asked for from Them?	
JOHN	sympathy for Suzy	not as much as he wants	yes	J: "that's what I thought you'd ask."
BILLY	approval	yes	?	E: "I feel the same about you."
SUZY	not to say no to her	sometimes - not always	some	D: "I don't know what you mean."
BILLY	What Did Each Person Ask You For?	Do You Think You Can Give It to Them?	Do You Think You Can Get What You Asked for from Them?	
JOHN	my friendship without interfering with my life	yes	yes	
MARY	being able to be angry	yes - not right away	yes	E: "I can't tell when I'm angry."
SUZY	stop teasing her	she wasn't serious - but I won't	not much right away	D: (Doesn't hear that she's serious)
SUZY	What Did Each Person Ask You For?	Do You Think You Can Give It to Them?	Do You Think You Can Get What You Asked for from Them?	
JOHN	?	yes	?	
MARY	to be more helpful	a little bit	yes	E: (nods)
BILLY	to understand him	sort of	yes	E: (looks spacy, nods)

Key: J = Joke　D = Denial　HA = Hidden Agenda　E = Evasion

Appendix 2

Asking Chart   Name: **SMITH**

	1	2	3	4	5	6
	Risk Taking	Listening	Ability to Get	Straight Talking	Straight Responding	Pos. Contact w. ea. other
	Does person ask directly for something for self?	Does Col. 1 on Question Cards=verbal request from others?	Does Col. 3 on Question Cards=verbal response from others?	Does verbal request = request written on Want Cards?	Does Col. 2 on Question Cards=verbal response?	Is verbal response affirmative?
JOHN	////	////	////	////	////	////
MARY	No	Yes	1/2	Yes	Yes	Yes
BILLY	Yes	Yes	Yes	Yes	Yes	Yes
SUZY	No	No	Yes	Yes	No	No
MARY	////	////	////	////	////	////
JOHN	Yes	Yes	Yes	1/2	1/2	Yes
BILLY	Yes	No	Yes	Yes	No	No
SUZY	Yes	Yes	Yes	Yes	No	No
BILLY	////	////	////	////	////	////
JOHN	Yes	Yes	Yes	Yes	Yes	Yes
MARY	Yes	Yes	No	Yes	1/2	1/2
SUZY	Yes	Yes	Yes	1/2	Yes	1/2
SUZY	////	////	////	////	////	////
JOHN	No	No	Yes	Yes	Yes	No
MARY	Yes	Yes	No	Yes	Yes	Yes
BILLY	Yes	Yes	No	1/2	1/2	Yes
Total	9	9	8.5	10.5	8.5	6
	75%	75%	70%	88% AV: 79%	70%	50%

FAMILY BONANZA

See filled-in "Smith" working sheets:
  Bonanza Card Charts, page 163;
  Bonanza Tape Charts, page 164;
  Special Notes to Reader on Filling out the Bonanza Tape Charts, page 161.

Step 1. Make and fill out the Bonanza Card Charts. Write all the items on the individuals' cards on *Cards Summary,* and the *Final Items* on the *Final Card* — i.e., how the family will spend the money. Also note any nonrequests for self — i.e., items written by a member on a card but never mentioned during the negotiating time.

Step 2. Make Bonanza Tape Charts:
a. *Item Analysis* will chart all the negotiations that directly involve the items members want to spend the money on. Make seven columns:
   Items (in the order they are mentioned)
   F/P (Is the item a Fantasy [F] or a Practicality [P]?)
   Who First (Who is the first person to mention the item — how many times does he/she subsequently mention it?)
   Who Supports (Which other members support that person in negotiating for that item — how many times?)
   Who Opposes (Which other members clearly and straightforwardly oppose that item — how many times?)
   Who Says Nothing
   Who Gets (Which members "get what they want," i.e., write an item on their individual card and have the family agree to it on the final family card, whether or not the member has negotiated for it?
b. *General Negotiations* will list, by individuals, the number of times each makes a general negotiation, supports a general negotiation, opposes a general negotiation, or uses any Negative Mechanisms within the general part of the conversation. By "general" negotiations we mean any negotiating not directly connected with items: for example, John says,

"We'd better make some decisions, our time is almost up," and Mary responds, "You're right. . . ." John makes a general negotiation here, Mary makes a general negotiation support.

c. *Negotiation Summary* is a total of the first chart and the *General Negotiations* list, showing the number of negotiations and Negative Mechanisms of individual members. It also shows the number of the individuals' *Hidden Agendas, Nonrequests for Self,* and *Reneges.*
Make eleven columns:
  N (for *Negotiations* — for item and general)
  N_2 (for *Negotiation Supports* — for item and general)
  O (for *Flat Oppositions* — for item and general)
  Says Nothing (for who says nothing — for item)
  Mechanisms (for *Negative Mechanisms* — for item and general)
  F (for *Fantasies* negotiated for)
  P (for *Practicalities* negotiated for)
  HA (for *Hidden Agendas*)
  Nonrequests (from the *Cards Summary,* for items written on card but not verbalized during negotiation time; from the *Item Analysis,* for asking only once and getting no response or for failure to speak for own items if someone else negotiates for same items)
  Reneges (for refusing to sign the final family card without giving fair warning ahead of time)

Step 3. Fill out Bonanza Tape Charts as you listen to the tape. Use our "Special Notes to Reader on Filling out the Bonanza Tape Charts" as a guide.
Use the following key:
  N = Negotiations, i.e., members' initiative efforts to get what they want, or to further the general negotiating process.
  N_2 = *Negotiation Supports*
  O = Flat Oppositions
  M = Negative Mechanisms

F = an item that is a *Fantasy* (e.g., a yearlong trip)
P = an item that is a *Practicality* (e.g., a new washing machine)

These Bonanza Tape Charts, unlike the charts in any other exercise, will include on them everything the family says during the ten-minute negotiating period — all of the verbal interactions, positive and negative.

On the Smith family charts, page 164, line 1 on the *Item Analysis* shows, for instance, that Suzy mentions "vacation," giving her an *F* for fantasy, and an *N* for negotiating for what she wants. She mentions vacation twice more during the negotiating, giving her two more *N*'s, a total of three. John gets two *N*'s for supporting Suzy's vacation. Mary has written "vacation" on her card, so that her three supports of Suzy are also negotiations for what she wants for herself — therefore, Mary gets three *N*'s. (Mary is in the *Who Supports* column here only because Suzy has mentioned "vacation" first.) Nobody ever opposes Suzy's vacation, so the *Who Opposes* column is blank. Billy never says anything one way or another when the vacation is being discussed, so his name is in the *Says Nothing* column. The *Who Gets* column is blank because the family, on the *Final Card,* does not opt to spend money on Suzy's idea of a vacation but on a yearlong trip, where Suzy does get credit, as it is close enough in spirit to her "vacation."

Step 4. Fill out Negative Mechanisms Sheet.

Fill out this sheet as you have in the other exercises, noting the total number of times family members use Negative Mechanisms.

At the end of the tape, add the number of *M*'s (Negative Mechanisms) for each person from the Negative Mechanisms Sheet to the ones for each person in *General Negotiations*, and enter the total on the *Negotiation Summary* chart (p. 164) beside the name of the member. In this way you can learn how a family gets messed up while they are trying to negotiate. In the Smith family, we found that John placates, Suzy distracts, Mary puts down, and Billy evades.

Make notes about these on the back of the sheet.

Step 5. Fill out Skills Sheet:

a. *Straight Talking/Responding:* Average the scores of i and ii, below:
   i. Total the family's N's, N_2's, and O's. Divide this number by the family's total N's, N_2's, O's, and M's;
   ii. Total the family's N_2's and O's and M's.
   SCORE: 5 = 100%; 4 = 80%; 3 = 60%; 2 = 40%; 1 = 20%; 0 = 0%.

b. *Listening:*
   i. Total the family *Says Nothings*. Divide that number by: the number of items verbalized, multiplied by (the number of family members minus 1);
   ii. Use the unitary complement of this number. That is, subtract the final answer from 100%. In the Smith family, there are 14 *Says Nothings*. We divide 14 by: the number of items verbalized in negotiating (11) multiplied by (the number of people minus 1) or 3; 14 divided by (11 times 3) is 14 divided by 33, or 42%. Subtracting this 42% from 100%, we have the unitary complement — 58%. The score, using the conversion formula, is then 3.
   SCORE: 5 = 100%; 4 = 80%; 3 = 60%; 2 = 40%; 1 = 20%; 0 = 0%

c. *Ability to Get What You Want:*
   i. Total the number of items the family gets on the *Final Card*. Divide this number by the number of items the family mentions in negotiating that are written on all their individual cards. The Smiths have 6 items on their *Final Card*. They mention 11 items that they have written on their individual cards; 6 divided by 11 is 54%. (Smith score, rounded off, is 3.)
   SCORE: 5 = 100%; 4 = 80%; 3 = 60%; 2 = 40%; 1 = 20%; 0 = 0%.

   ii. Total the number of Nonrequests for Self from the Negotiation Summary. (On p. 164, the Smiths have 3.)
   SCORE: 5 = 100%; 4 = 80%; 3 = 60%; 2 = 40%; 1 = 20%; 0 = 0%.

window. She worries about money and had "savings" on her own list. What are they for?

Line 4. Billy changes the subject to an "addition to the summer cabin," a dream of his mother's which both have written down. Then ensues a battle about Suzy's bad behavior — not helping, at the cabin or at home — and Mary's feeling that she is overworked there because of the primitive conditions. John comes in supporting the addition and placating Mary and Suzy. Mary also negotiates for the addition many times, now and later when John says he wants to pay off the loan on the cabin. Her *Hidden Agenda* here is that she is angry at John as she does not get any real help there from him even though he tells the children to be helpful. He in fact does nothing to help. Her anger comes out at Suzy. Mary *never* mentions in this or any other exchange her washing machine for the cabin which she wrote down; we gave her an *NR* on the *Cards Summary*.

Appendix 2

Bonanza Card Charts   Name: __SMITH__

Amount of Check:

Cards Summary

JOHN	MARY	BILLY	SUZY
pay cabin loan (2,000)	add on to cabin	college	big trip
college (15,000)	winter vacation	add to cabin	yacht
yearlong family trip (6,000)	pay bills	individual frivolity $500 each	
charity (2,000)	fix car	savings	
	savings		
	washing machine for cabin (NR)		

Key: NR = Nonrequest for Self

Final Card

Final Items	$	Fantasy	Practicality
yearlong family trip	$10,000	$10,000	
college	6,000		$6,000
add to cabin	3,000	3,000	
pay bills	3,000		3,000
charity	2,000		2,000
frivolities	1,000	1,000	
__6__ Items Totals	$25,000	$14,000	$11,000

Bonanza Tape Charts   Name: SMITH

Item Analysis

Lines:	Items in Order	F/P	Who First	Who Supports	Who Opposes	Who Says Nothing	Who Gets
1	vacation	F	Suzy NNN	John N₂ N₂ Mary NNN		Billy	
2	yacht (NR)	F	Suzy N			John Billy Mary	
3	college (HA)	P	Billy NNN	John NNN	Suzy O	Mary	John Billy
4	cabin addition (HA)	F	Billy N	John N₂N₂ Mary NNNN	Suzy OOO		Billy Mary
5	frivolities (HA)	F	Billy NNN	John N₂ N₂ Mary N₂ N₂ Suzy N₂ N₂N₂N₂ N₂			Billy (4)
6	savings	P	Billy N	Mary N Suzy N		John	
7	pay cabin loan (NR)	P	John N			Billy Mary Suzy	
8	yr. long trip (HA)	F	John NNN NNN	Billy N₂ Suzy N₂ N₂	Mary O		John Suzy
9	charity (HA)	P	John NN	Mary N₂N₂	Suzy OO	Billy John	
10	fix car (HA)	P	Mary NN	John N₂		Billy Suzy	
11	pay bills	P	Mary NN NNN	John N₂ N₂		Billy Suzy	Mary
	Total Items						

General Negotiations: JOHN: NN M N NN M   BILLY: N₂ M
MARY: N N₂ N₂ M   SUZY: N₂ M M

Negotiation Summary

Names	N	N₂	O	Says Nothing	Mechanisms	F	P	HA	Nonrequests (both pages)	Reneges
JOHN	16	10	0	2	5	1	2	0	1	0
MARY	17	6	1	3	6	0	2	2	1	0
BILLY	8	2	0	6	2	2	2	2	0	0
SUZY	4	8	6	3	7	2	0	1	1	0
FAMILY TOTAL:	45	26	7	14	20	5	6	6	3	0

Key: N = Negotiations
      N₂ = Negotiation Supports
      M = Negative Mechanisms –
          placating, complaints,
          jokes, denials, evasions,
          interruptions, etc.
          Scored as what they are
          on Mechanism Sheet.

      F = Fantasies
      P = Practicalities
      O = Flat Opposition
      HA = Hidden Agenda
      R = Reneges
      NR = Nonrequests for Self

Appendix 3

The Smith Family

History Taking (page 1)   Name: **SMITH**

I. Ask Each Family Member: (10 minutes total)

Each of you please share with me why you are here.
John: perspective on family process Mary: new information from outside view Billy, Suzy: don't know - John decides they should come
Is anyone important not here?
All agree grandparents important, but not part of nuclear family.
What is your occupation?
John: School psychologist
What is your yearly family income?
$25,000
What is your religion?
Methodist

II. Ask Husband and Wife about Their Grandparents: (5 minutes total)

	Husband Paternal Grandparents		Wife Paternal Grandparents	
	Grandfather	Grandmother	Grandfather	Grandmother
where born	Canada	Canada	?	?
when die	1938	1935	1943	1956
what kind of person was he/she	no one in fam. liked him. Mean	"saintly"	?	dressed well

	Maternal Grandparents		Maternal Grandparents	
	Grandfather	Grandmother	Grandfather	Grandmother
where born	Oregon	California	Southwest	?
when die	1940	alive	1949-50	1954-55
what kind of person was he/she	Nice - John named after him	lovely - down-to-earth	smoked a lot	snored - good sense of humor

Appendix 3

History Taking (page 2)   Name: SMITH

III. Ask Husband and Wife about Their Parents: (15 minutes total)

	Husband Father	Husband Mother	Wife Father	Wife Mother
still alive (when die)	(1969)	alive	alive	alive
marriage date	exact date unclear		1925	
divorces # marriages	none	none	none	none
occupation unemployment	Insurance Salesman	nurse	Jack of all trades - jobs insecure	drafts-woman
abortions miscarriages		several abortions		none
religion	nominal	protestants	none	strict Baptist
how did they get along	very affectionate mother dependent on father		"o.k."	
how did they show caring	took family on picnics	comforted	father teased neither showed direct caring	
what was their sex life like	good - private		"no sex life"	
how did they show anger	teased kids no open fights - fought in bedroom	w. each other	both controlled "never angry"	
physical violence	spanked kids hard	none	none	none
alcohol	none	none	not allowed in house	
physical illness	none	none	none	none
emotional problems - seek help	none	none	none	none
who made decisions	mostly father			mother
who made rules	father			mother
who handled money	both worked both shared #		both father paid bills	

History Taking (page 3)   Name: **SMITH**

IV. Ask Husband and Wife about Their Upbringing: (20 minutes total)

	Husband	Wife
date of birth	1936	1936
planned/ unplanned	unplanned	unplanned
sibs birth order	John oldest - 2 brothers	Mary youngest - 3 much older sisters
how did you get along with parents	Mother - good fought with father	Mother - O.K. father - great
how did you get what you wanted	by achieving - warmth freely given in family	by demanding, sulking
how were you punished	spanked by father	never punished "good kid"
how did you show anger	didn't	never at father yelled at others
how did you show physical affection	hugged + kissed all	hugged + kissed all combed M's + F's hair
what do you think your family expected of you	achieve be fair	go to college
emotional problems	teenage rebellion against father	upset by indecent exposure age 4 - family frightened
illness accidents	none	none
problems of sibs	none	none
what was most significant death	favorite uncle	none
how was that death handled	mutual comforting in family	
how did you feel about yourself growing up	good, but had to compete	confused popular overweight
how do you feel about yourself now	good, with occasional feelings of inadequacy	good most of the time

Appendix 3

History Taking (page 4)   Name: SMITH

V. Ask Husband and Wife about Their Life Together: (20 minutes total)

	Husband	Wife
date of marriage/ former marriages	June 1957 — No —	
what attracted you to him/her	she was pretty, vivacious	he was cute, tall
what made you decide to marry	father grumbled — I was "too young"	we were expected to — childhood sweethearts
did "honeymoon" live up to expectations	spontaneous, wonderful very funny embarrassments	
what was your sex life like then	good — fun — joyous — warm	
what is your sex life like now	still good — very much a part of life	
did you discuss having kids	yes	yes
were children planned/unplanned ask re each child	Billy: "very planned" — both wanted a child Suzy: "a happy mistake"	
miscarriages		none
abortions		none
did your relationship change once you had kids	less time together, but no essential change.	I needed less support from John
friends - social life	house always open to friends — casual entertaining + outdoor activities	
how do you show anger to each other	hold it in, then lecture	argue, yell
how do you show caring to each other	hug, hold hands, listen to her problems	hug, hold hands, cook his favorite foods
what are the rules in the family now	don't need specific rules — both insist on "honesty" and "fairness"	
taboo subjects in family	none	jealousy
problems with alcohol	none	none
have you ever considered separation or divorce	big fight when children small — resolved satisfactorily. Now very close.	

History Taking (page 5)   Name: __SMITH__

VI. Ask Each Child about His/Her Life: (10 minutes each)

BILLY

date of birth	July 12, 1958
how do you get along with sibs	used to fight with Suzy - fight less now
illness accidents	none
how are you doing in school	very well
friends	lots, make them easily
sex education	father, school, friends
drugs/alcohol	no problems
moving	we've moved a lot but "not that sad" to lose friends
what are the rules in this family	no specific rules
how are you punished/ who punishes you	spanked by both parents when little - no punishments now
how do you think your parents get along-- show caring to each other show anger to each other	get along well hug each other tell each other when angry (afraid when parents had big fight)
how do you show caring and to whom	hug father
how do you show anger and to whom	sulk
how do you get what you want in your family	"ask, take by force, appeal to hierarchy"
do you think there are taboo subjects in family	sex, drugs
do you think you have a special role in this family	parents both proud of me - be myself - honest, fair, friendly
how do you feel about yourself	really good

Appendix 3

History Taking (page 5)   Name: SMITH

VI. Ask Each Child about His/Her Life: (10 minutes each)

Suzy

date of birth	August 11, 1961
how do you get along with sibs	friends with Billy - I really like him
illness accidents	many small accidents; stitches, broken arm. Almost kidnapped in park age 3 - still scares her. (Parents vague re kidnapping)
how are you doing in school	average, but I love it
friends	lots
sex education	father, science class
drugs/alcohol	no problems
moving	don't like moving - miss friends. Parents don't discuss moving with me
what are the rules in this family	keep my room clean
how are you punished/ who punishes you	used to be spanked by father now sent to room, grounded
how do you think your parents get along-- show caring to each other show anger to each other	get along very well talk things out together Mother yells; Father harsh but calm.
how do you show caring and to whom	tell them I love them, hug father, Mother hard to hug
how do you show anger and to whom	sulk, ignore people, scream
how do you get what you want in your family	ask, threaten, beg for approval
do you think there are taboo subjects in family	Billy won't talk about sex
do you think you have a special role in this family	be the baby be perfect for Mother be who I am for father
how do you feel about yourself	don't like being new kid in school, want to be like Billy, he's neat.

When a Family Needs Therapy

History Taking Analysis   Name: **SMITH**

Husband: Name: **JOHN**   Date of Birth: **1936**

Family Background: Rising middle-class Protestant. Patriarchal sex roles. Both parents worked. Affectionate, warm, stable, fairly open about sex, money, death.

Personal History: Oldest (unplanned) of three boys. Expected to achieve, and did. Father disciplined by spanking, mother comforted. Felt he had to compete with father, rebelled as teenager. Never showed anger. Felt generally good about self.

Wife: Name: **MARY**   Date of Birth: **1936**

Family Background: "Remembers little" about grandparents. Lower middle-class. Father insecure in job. Mother strict Baptist, worked. Pleasure feelings inhibited. Anger very tightly controlled. Parents had "no sex life." Money was source of anger. Alcohol, sex taboo. Mother dominated family.

Personal History: Youngest of 4 girls (mistake?). Expected to go to college. Never punished—got what she wanted by demanding, sulking. Got affection from both parents. Confused as teenager, feels quite good about self now. Note incident of indecent exposure age 4—never dealt with. Similar episode with Suzy. (over)

Appendix 3

History Taking Analysis (page 2)

Child #1: Name: BILLY   Date of Birth: July 12, 1958

Personal History: Much sibling jealousy in past, less now. Generally friendly, healthy, successful, popular boy, but cannot show any negative feelings. Living up to Father's and Mother's expectations to be honest, fair, friendly. Feels good. Close to father, having some trouble separating from mother, as she wants to hang on.

Child #2: Name: SUZY   Date of Birth: Aug. 11, 1961

Personal History: Suzy admires Billy, wants more attention from him, goes about getting it in baby ways. Problems with mother - feels put upon that she can't get her approval or affection. Used to be punished by father spanking, now sent to room. Shows anger by screaming, sulking, gets what she wants in nearly the same way. Accident prone. Physically affectionate with father. Feels parents expect her to be baby. Acts like baby. Feels only "fair" about self. Note incident in park age 3 (similar to Mary's) never dealt with by family.

Skills Sheet   Name: __SMITH__

                            # Family Members: __4__

Skills	Exercises					Aver. for Skill	Skill-Grouped Score (Average)
	House	Roles	Prob	Askg	Bon		
Straight Talking/ Responding				4	3.5	3.75	Communication
Listening				4	3	3.5	
Shared Facts, Meanings, Values		4				4.0	3.75
Risk Taking			5	4		4.5	Problem Solving
Openness intra Family	5		1			3.0	
Negotiating					3.5	3.5	3.60
Decision Making					4	4.0	
Responsibility		2			4	3.0	
Positive Contact with Each Other	4	4		2.5		3.5	Family Self-Esteem
Ability to Play	4	3.5			3.5	3.75	
Ability to Get What You Want	5			3.5	3	3.8	3.66
Accepting Individual Differences	5	3			5	4.3	Receptivity to Growth and Change
Limit Setting	0					0	
Internally Chosen Roles		4				4.0	3.15
Openness to the Outside	5		5		3	4.3	
Average Score for Each Exercise	4	3.4	3.7	3.6	3.6	3.6	

Notes on Each Skill:

<u>Straight Talking</u>: All straight except for Mary, who is equivocal, or "doesn't remember" past. Bonanza score lowered by hidden agenda, and Mary and Suzy not stating preferences.

<u>Listening</u>: Good except when anger is being hidden.

<u>Shared Facts</u>, <u>Risktaking</u>, <u>Openness</u>: All open about

facts and all feelings except anger.

Negotiating: Marred by John's placating.

Decision Making: All members willing to make agreements.

Responsibility: Low score in area of job roles — sexist job differentiation.

Positive Contact: Members mobile and able to relate positively. Though Mary and Billy dump anger on Suzy.

Ability to Play: High family energy level during house drawing. Family agrees to spend money on "frivolities" in Bonanza.

Ability to Get: Mary's difficulty in saying what she wants lowers the family score in Bonanza.

Accepting Individual Differences, Internally Chosen Roles: High, except for sexist stereotyping.

Limit Setting: Great difficulty setting limits — especially on Suzy.

Openness to The Outside: The family is intellectually and emotionally receptive to the world at large.

Negative Mechanisms Sheet   Name: **SMITH**

Negative Mechanisms	Exercises					Total
	House	Roles	Prob	Askg	Bon	
Errors						0
Unnecessary Questions and Complaints re ex.	7	19	3	13	2	44
"It's Impossible" "I Won't Play"						0
General Complaining						0
Evasions			2	10	4	16
Denials				2		2
Double Messages						0
Answering for Others						0
Speaking for Others	7		1	3		11
Giving Orders						0
Placating	2	3	2	4	4	15
Blaming			1	1	1	3
Sarcastic Remarks						0
Inappropriate Jokes			1	3		4
Distractions	8	5		1	3	17
Interruptions			2	1	3	6
Defensive Long-Talking						0
Putdowns	3	10	3	2	3	21
Self-Putdowns	1	4		2		7
Lies						0
Bribes						0
Threats						0
Defiance/Rulebreaking						0
Loud Screaming						0
Fake Placating						0
Other:						0
Total for Each Exercise:	28	41	15	42	20	146

Major Factors Inhibiting Family Growth:
(list highest totals)
Unnecessary Questions
Evasions
Speaking for Others
Placating
Distractions
Interruptions
Putdowns

Family is Largely Free of:
(list lowest totals)
"It's Impossible"
General Complaining
Double Messages
Answering for Others
Giving Orders
Sarcastic Remarks
Defensive Long-Talking
Lies
Bribes
Threats
Defiance/Rulebreaking
Loud Screaming
Fake Placating
Denials
Blaming
Inappropriate Joking
Self-Putdowns

(over)

Appendix 3

Negative Mechanisms Notes:

House: Suzy asks most of the <u>unnecessary questions</u>, is answered by John. (Playing baby?) Mary + Suzy do <u>takeovers</u> - Mary twice on John, once on Suzy. Suzy's initial takeover - drawing house outline while others are trying to negotiate - is met with silence. She proceeds with 7 <u>distractions</u> - lying across paper, sitting on John. No limits are set. Mary shows anger by giving her a push.

Roles: Suzy asks <u>questions</u> about all the roles she chooses. Suzy and Billy <u>put</u> each other <u>down</u> via cards. Mary sees self as Blamer, doesn't reject it; Suzy doesn't reject Distracter and Victim; John doesn't reject Placater. They seem stuck in a system.

Problems: All state real problems, but Billy and Mary try to scapegoat Suzy. John takes no direct part in this - he <u>placates</u>, <u>evades</u>. Suzy <u>interrupts</u>, <u>puts down</u> Billy. Mary <u>jokes</u> at John's problem, Suzy <u>interrupts</u>. When Suzy asks for more privileges, Mary says she's untrustworthy. John <u>placates</u> between the two.

Asking: Suzy has 6 <u>evasions</u>, 4 in communication with John. She doesn't know how to relate to him, perhaps because he and Mary are in such conflict about her. Mary and Billy share 3 of their 4 <u>evasions</u> with each other. They are in conflict about distance. John and Mary both <u>joke</u> at each other's requests. Suzy asks many <u>questions</u> about the directions.

Bonanza: John placates arguments between Suzy and Mary. Mary uses cabin discussion to <u>put down</u> Suzy. Billy <u>evades</u> some questions. Suzy <u>interrupts</u> and <u>distracts</u>.

Family Dynamics Sheet   Name: SMITH

History Taking:
Family seems largely free of dysfunctional dynamics - warm, open, supportive. Mary is vague about her family of origin - some secrets? Neither family of origin open about anger.

Draw a House:
Family boundaries open to outsiders - easy access egress to + from house. Mary tries to control others (power) by drawing John, Suzy's mess, but ends up not clearly defining herself except through kitchen, and outside the house in pool.

Role Card Game:
Sex-stereotyped roles. Mary does most of the housework; little responsibility is taught to the children. John emotionally supportive by saying positive roles belong to all of them.

Family Problems:
Billy and Mary try to scapegoat Suzy - anger not allowed elsewhere. John + Mary show undercover anger at each other. John complains he has to do too much to keep peace, has no time for self. Mary laughs at him, shuts him off.

Asking for What you Want:
Hidden Agenda: Mary to John: "I want your love forever" (i.e. never leave me, never show me your anger). Both parents joke at each other's requests hiding anger. John angry at Mary's behavior to Suzy. Mary's assumption that Billy wants more of her may reflect her inability to let go of him.

Family Bonanza:
Sexist attitudes about worksharing. Males placate + evade problems of "women's work". John gets what he wants (power) by being nice. Suzy's distracting behavior gets her nothing for her own. Mary shows sideways anger about their not having enough money.

Family Sculpture:
Warmth, mutual support. John assumes power position. Sexist attitude. Males stronger than females.

(over)

Nonverbal Notes on Exercises

History Taking:

All seem open, welcoming. Suzy and Billy walk around a lot, get food from kitchen. Relaxed, warm atmosphere in house.

Draw a House:

All generally mobile during drawing — Suzy distractingly so. Billy tends to work quietly, apart from others. Suzy barricades self in chair after drawing, with paper rolled in front of her.

Role Card Game:

John talks non-stop. Mary's cards are a disorganized mess. Suzy drops cards on floor, distracts. Billy neat, orderly, accurate.

Family Problems:

All slouched. Suzy curled up in wing chair, wiggling. Mary covers face with hand. Billy looks spacy, depressed.

Asking for What You Want:

Billy leaves room "for a drink" just as we start. Suzy has a hard time relating to her parents — giggly and nervous with Mary, spacy with John.

Family Bonanza:

All relaxed most of the time — lots of genial laughing.

Family Sculpture:

All relate to the idea of sculpture — mobile and inventive about positions, easily make physical contact with one another.

Summary Sheet   SMITH

Inherited Family Process:

No serious family background problems. Physical affection between parents and children open on both sides. Anger repressed on both sides. Both saw parents as not equally sharing responsibility and power.

Present Family Process:

Skills: Generally high in all areas, particularly in communication. Low on limit setting. Members are close, but hooked into one another's feelings; they use overresponsibility for one another as a form of control.

Dynamics: Some alliances: Mary/Billy, and John/Suzy. Sexism cherished by all. Near scapegoating of Suzy. Anger expressed only by females, and in indirect ways — pouting, sulking.

"Contract" between Husband and Wife:

Traditional, romantic: "We will be highschool sweethearts, in love forever. John will be strong, Mary will be loving and helpful."

(over)

Appendix 3

Summary Sheet (page 2)

Sculpture Comments:

Very moving sculpture. Took ½ hour. Family open to nonverbal exploration. Issues of Mary's dependency on John, John's need for space, Suzy's need to be between John and Mary, be baby. Billy a bit detached.

Stated Present Problems:

Suzy acting up, not able to get along well at home, school.

Problems as I See Them:

Anger between parents comes out on Suzy. Sexism, infantalizing of females in family. Overresponsibility for each other's feelings. Billy isolated in "good son" role.

Family's Goals:

To be able to enjoy each other more, and to help Suzy.

Contract Needed with Family:

Agreement from whole family to meet several times to work on underlying anger, overresponsibility. Agreement from parents to meet several times to clarify relationship, work on Mary's giving up female power/dependency games.

TABLE #1 NEGATIVE MECHANISM FREQUENCIES

	\multicolumn{7}{c}{TOTALS FOR INTERVIEWS II, III}	
	\multicolumn{7}{c}{FAMILIES}	EACH
NEGATIVE MECHANISMS	A	B	C	D	E	F	G	MECH.
Unnecessary Questions	56	20	27	14	29	38	32	216
Nonanswers	4	0	0	0	1	0	4	9
"I Don't Knows"	0	0	0	0	0	0	0	0
Lies	0	0	0	2	0	0	4	6
Evasions	0	4	2	18	18	27	18	87
Denials	4	5	7	10	17	20	7	70
Reneges	5	0	2	2	1	4	0	14
Discrepancies Fam. Ans. to Common Questions	0	0	0	2	0	2	0	4
Discrepancies Verbal vs. Written	1	0	0	1	3	1	0	6
Errors	0	3	3	5	1	17	20	49
Answering for Others	1	2	0	0	0	1	1	5
Speaking for Others	17	22	5	4	16	13	24	101
Interpreting	1	6	0	0	5	0	0	12
Separating	6	0	0	0	0	15	0	21
Placating	0	3	5	20	2	6	9	45
Assumption Making	0	5	4	4	1	11	3	28
Blaming	1	0	0	0	2	8	11	22
Inappropriate Jokes	4	20	2	13	11	2	4	56
Distractions	16	6	32	0	7	9	23	103
Interruptions	6	25	60	4	90	45	36	266
Complaints	2	3	2	1	0	0	27	34
Putdowns	41	19	14	8	85	73	88	328
Self-Putdowns	5	0	5	6	12	45	6	79
Nonrequests for Self	15	0	2	7	28	7	29	88
Expectations	2	1	4	0	0	2	0	9
Secrets, Myths, Taboos	0	0	3	6	17	3	14	43
Collusions	0	10	16	25	26	24	29	130
Double Messages	8	0	0	0	0	0	0	8
Giving Orders	0	18	0	0	21	0	0	39
Defensive Long-talking	0	0	4	0	0	0	0	4
Rule Anxiety	0	0	0	0	0	10	0	10
Controlling Numbers	0	0	0	0	0	18	0	18
Physical Threats	0	0	0	0	0	0	6	6
Rules Dictating	0	0	0	0	0	0	19	19
"I Won't Play"	0	0	0	0	0	0	20	20
Bribes	0	0	0	0	0	0	12	12
"It's Impossible"	0	0	0	0	0	0	27	27
Fake Validating/Complying	0	0	0	0	0	0	35	35

(TABLE #1 CONTINUED)

	TOTALS FOR INTERVIEWS II, III							
	FAMILIES							EACH
NEGATIVE MECHANISMS	A	B	C	D	E	F	G	MECH.
Warnings	0	0	0	0	0	0	9	9
Sarcasm	0	0	0	0	0	0	9	9
Defiance/"No!"	0	0	0	0	0	0	25	25
Rule Breaking	0	0	0	0	0	0	3	3
Whining	0	0	0	0	0	0	22	22
"Cut It Out"	0	0	0	0	0	0	4	4
Individual Screams	0	0	0	0	0	0	15	15
Foul Language	0	0	0	0	0	0	13	13

TABLE #2 SKILLS SCORES FOR EACH FAMILY

SKILLS	A	B	C	D	E	F	G	SKILL AVERAGE
Straight Talk/ Responding	4.5* (1)**	3.5 (2,3,4)	3.5 (2,3,4)	2.5 (5)	3.5 (2,3,4)	2.45 (6)	1.7 (7)	3.09
Listening	3.5 (3,4)	3.8 (1)	3.7 (2)	2.8 (6)	3.2 (5)	3.5 (3,4)	1.0 (7)	3.07
Shared Facts, Meanings, Values	4.2 (2)	3.8 (4)	3.9 (3)	4.6 (1)	3.5 (5)	2.5 (6)	2.2 (7)	3.53
Risk Taking	4.5 (1)	3.75 (3)	4.4 (2)	2.4 (6)	3.2 (4)	2.9 (5)	1.4 (7)	3.22
Openness Intra Family	4.2 (1)	1.9 (5)	2.1 (4)	1.75 (6)	3.0 (2,3)	3.0 (2,3)	1.0 (7)	2.42
Negotiating	4.2 (1)	3.8 (3)	3.75 (4)	3.25 (6)	4.0 (2)	3.4 (5)	1.0 (7)	3.34
Decision Making	4.5 (4,5)	5.0 (1,2,3)	5.0 (1,2,3)	4.5 (4,5)	5.0 (1,2,3)	2.5 (6)	0.5 (7)	3.86
Responsibility	2.5 (2,3)	3.0 (1)	2.0 (4,5)	2.0 (4,5)	0.6 (7)	1.75 (6)	2.5 (2,3)	2.05
Positive Contact with Each Other	3.75 (2)	3.8 (1)	2.0 (4,5)	3.3 (3)	2.0 (4,5)	1.9 (6)	0.6 (7)	2.48
Ability to Play	3.25 (2)	3.3 (1)	0.3 (7)	2.9 (3)	1.0 (5)	2.3 (4)	0.8 (6)	1.98
Ability to Get What You Want	3.6 (2)	3.7 (1)	3.0 (3,4)	2.5 (5)	3.0 (3,4)	1.8 (6)	0.5 (7)	2.59
Accepting Individual Differences	3.0 (1)	2.8 (2,3)	2.8 (2,3)	2.75 (4)	2.3 (6)	2.4 (5)	1.8 (7)	2.55
Limit Setting	3.25 (4)	3.75 (3)	0.5 (7)	4.5 (2)	2.7 (5)	5.0 (1)	0.75 (6)	2.92
Internally Chosen Roles	3.5 (2)	3.6 (1)	2.4 (5)	2.6 (3,4)	2.6 (3,4)	0.5 (7)	2.3 (6)	2.50
Openness to the Outside	4.75 (1)	3.5 (2)	2.8 (4)	2.4 (6)	3.1 (3)	2.6 (5)	1.65 (7)	2.97
Family Average	3.81 (1)	3.53 (2)	2.81 (5)	2.98 (3)	2.85 (4)	2.57 (6)	1.31 (7)	2.84

*Upper numbers are Skills scores.
**Lower numbers in parentheses are rank ordered over families.

Bibliography

ALCOHOL

Coudert, Jo, *The Alcoholic in Your Life* (New York: Stein & Day, 1972).
Steiner, Claud, *Games Alcoholics Play* (New York: Ballantine Books, 1971).

ANGER

Bach, George R., and Peter Wyden, *The Intimate Enemy* (New York: Morrow, 1968).

ANTHROPOLOGICAL/SOCIOLOGICAL FAMILY STUDIES

Bateson, Gregory, and Margaret Mead, *Balinese Character: A Photographic Analysis* (New York: Special Publications of the New York Academy of Sciences, Vol. II, 1942).
Bettleheim, Bruno, *Children of the Dream* (New York: Avon 1971).
Houriet, Robert, *Getting Back Together* (New York: Coward, McCann & Geohegan, 1971).
Sidel, Ruth, *Women and Child Care in China: A Firsthand Report* (New York: Hill & Wang, 1972).

BODY THEORY

Birdwhistell, Ray, *Kinesics and Context* (Philadelphia: University of Pennsylvania Press, 1970).
Fisher, Seymour, *Body Consciousness* (Englewood Cliffs, N.J.: Prentice-Hall, 1973).
Lowen, Alexander, *Betrayal of the Body* (New York: Macmillan, 1966).
Montagu, Ashley, *Touching: The Human Significance of the Skin* (New York: Columbia University Press, 1971).
Reich, Wilhelm, *Selected Writings: An Introduction to Orgonomy* (Toronto: Doubleday Canada, 1951).
Simeones, A.T.W., *Man's Presumptuous Brain* (New York: Dutton, 1960).

CHILDREN

Aries, Phillipe, *Centuries of Childhood: A Social History of Family Life* (New York: Vintage, 1962).
Axline, Virginia M., *Play Therapy* (New York: Ballantine, 1947).
Dennison, George, *The Lives of Children* (New York: Random House, 1969).
Erikson, Erik H., *Identity, Youth and Crisis* (New York: Norton, 1968).
Fraiberg, Selma H., *The Magic Years* (New York: Scribner's, 1959).
Freud, Anna, *The Psychoanalytical Treatment of Children* (New York: Schocken, 1971).
Gesell, Arnold, *The Child from Five to Ten* (New York: Harper, 1946).
Ginott, Haim, *Between Parent and Child* (New York: Macmillan, 1965).
Holt, John, *How Children Fail* (New York: Dell, 1964).
Kozol, Jonathan, *Death at an Early Age* (Boston: Houghton Mifflin, 1967).
Murphy, L. B., et al., *The Widening World of Childhood* (New York: Basic Books, 1962).
Piaget, Jean, *The Construction of Reality in the Child* (New York: Basic Books, 1954).

DEATH

Fanberg, Dan, "Preventive Therapy with Siblings of a Dying Child," *Journal of the American Association of Child Psychiatrists*, vol. 9, no. 4 (1970), pp. 644–668.
Grollman, Earl A., *Concerning Death* (Boston: Beacon Press, 1974).
———, *Talking About Death*, rev. ed. (Boston: Beacon Press, 1976).
Hinton, John, *Dying* (Harmondsworth, Middlesex, England: Penguin Books, 1967).
Hirschhorn, Theodora, "The Will to Live or the Will to Die," *Journal of Emotional Education*, vol. 8, no. 1 (1968), pp. 8–20.
Kubler-Ross, Elisabeth, *On Death and Dying* (New York: Macmillan, 1969).
———, *Questions on Death and Dying* (New York: Macmillan, 1974).
Menninger, Karl A., *Man Against Himself* (New York: Harcourt Brace & World, 1938).

DIVORCE

Despert, J. Louise, *Children of Divorce* (New York: Dolphin Books, 1962).
Grollman, Earl A., *Explaining Divorce to Children* (Boston: Beacon Press, 1969).
———, *Talking About Divorce* (Boston: Beacon Press, 1975).
Whitaker, Carl, and M. H. Miller, "A Reevaluation of 'Psychiatric Help' When Divorce Impends," *American Journal of Psychiatry*, vol. 126, no. 5 (1969), pp. 611–618.

EMOTIONAL ILLNESS

Barnes, Mary, and Joseph Berk, *Two Accounts of a Journey Through Madness* (New York: Harcourt Brace Jovanovich, 1971).
Green, Hannah, *I Never Promised You a Rose Garden* (New York: Holt, Rinehart & Winston, 1967).
Greenfeld, Josh, *A Child Called Noah* (New York: Holt, Rinehart & Winston, 1972).
Kesey, Ken, *One Flew over the Cuckoo's Nest* (New York: Viking, 1962).
Laing, R. D., *The Divided Self* (London: Tavistock Publications, 1959).
───, *Knots* (New York: Pantheon, 1970).
Ruitenbeek, Hendrik M., ed., *Going Crazy* (New York: Bantam Books, 1972).
Sechehaye, Marguerite, *Autobiography of a Schizophrenic Girl* (New York: Grune & Stratton, 1951).
Thigpen, Corbett H., and Hervey M. Cleckley, *The Three Faces of Eve* (New York: McGraw-Hill, 1957).

FAMILY THERAPY/FAMILY SYSTEM

Ackerman, Nathan, "The Role of the Family in the Emergence of Child Disorders," *Foundation of Child Psychiatry*, ed. Emanuel Miller (London: Pergamon Press Ltd., 1968, pp. 509–533).
───, *Treating the Troubled Family* (New York: Basic Books, 1968).
Bateson, Gregory, et al., *The Natural History of an Interview*, ed. N. McQuown (New York: Grune & Stratton, forthcoming).
Beels, C. C., and A. Ferber, "Family Therapy: A View," *Family Process*, vol. 8, no. 2 (1969), pp. 280–318.
Boszormenyi-Nagy, I., *Intensive Family Therapy*, ed. I. Boszormenyi-Nagy and J. Framo (New York: Harper & Row, 1965).
Carter, Elizabeth, and Thomas Fogarty, Workshop, McLean Hospital, Belmont, Mass.: Society for Family Therapy and Research, March 1,2, 1974.
Cooper, David, *The Death of the Family* (New York: Random House, 1970).
Duhl, Frederick J., David Kantor, and Bunny S. Duhl, "Learning, Space, and Action in Family Therapy: A Primer of Sculpture," *Techniques of Family Psychotherapy: A Primer*, ed. Donald A. Bloch (New York: Grune & Stratton, 1973).
Epstein, Nathan B., Vivian Rakoff, and John J. Sigal, "Working-Through in Conjoint Family Therapy," *American Journal of Psychotherapy*, vol. 21, no. 4 (October, 1967) pp. 782–790.
Ferber, Andrew, Marilyn Mendelsohn, and Augustus Napier, eds., *The Book of Family Therapy* (Boston: Houghton Mifflin, 1973).
Gerrish, Maddy, and Eileen Cooney, Training Course in Family Process and Therapy, Bedford, Mass.: March – July, 1973.

Haley, Jay, "Beginning and Experienced Family Therapists," *The Book of Family Therapy* (Boston: Houghton Mifflin, 1973).
———, *Strategies of Psychotherapy* (New York: Grune & Stratton, 1963).
Hamilton, Eleanor, *Partners in Love* (Cranbury, N.J.: A.S. Barnes, 1961).
Jungreis, J., *Psychotherapy for the Whole Family*, ed. A. Friedman (New York: Springer, 1965).
Kantor, David, and Frederick Duhl, Workshop, Boston: Boston Family Institute, June 10, 1973.
Laing, R. D., *The Politics of the Family* (New York: Pantheon, 1969).
———, and A. Esterson, *Sanity, Madness, and the Family* (New York: Basic Books, 1970).
La Perriere, Kitty, Workshop, Pine Manor Junior College, Brookline, Mass.: Human Resources Institute, May 3, 1974.
Lederer, William J., and Donald D. Jackson, *The Mirages of Marriage* (New York: Norton, 1968).
MacGregor, Robert, et al., *Multiple Impact Therapy with Families* (New York: Grune & Stratton, 1964).
Minuchin, Salvador, *Families and Family Therapy* (Cambridge, Mass.: Harvard University Press, 1974).
———, B. Montalvo, B. Guerney, B. Rosman, and F. Shumer, *Families of the Slums* (New York: Basic Books, 1967).
Napier, Augustus, and Carl Whitaker, "A Conversation About Co-Therapy," *The Book Of Family Therapy* (Boston: Houghton Mifflin, 1973), pp. 480–506.
Olsen, Kenneth J., "An Investigation of Scapegoating, Favoritism, and Self-Blame in Families," *Dissertation Abstracts*, vol. 29, no. 2-A (1968), pp. 484–485.
O'Neill, Nena, and George O'Neill, *Open Marriage* (New York: M. Evans, 1972).
Paul, Norman, and Joseph D. Bloom, "Multiple Family Therapy: Secrets and Scapegoating in Family Crisis," *International Journal Of Group Psychotherapy*, vol. 20, no. 1 (1970), pp. 37–47.
Prosky, Phoebe, Workshop, Boston: Ackerman Institute of New York, November 10, 1973.
Satir, Virginia, *Conjoint Family Therapy* (Palo Alto, Calif.: Science and Behavior Books, 1964).
———, *Peoplemaking* (Palo Alto, Calif.: Science and Behavior Books, 1972).
———, Workshop, Hofstra College, New York: Family Studies Unit, North Shore University Hospital, Manhasset, N.Y., January 26, 1974.
Warkentin, John, and Carl A. Whitaker, "The Secret Agenda of the Therapist Doing Couples Therapy," *Family Therapy and Disturbed Families*, ed. Gerald Zuk and I. Boszormenyi-Nagy

(Palo Alto, Calif.: Science and Behavior Books, 1967), pp. 239–243.

Watzlawick, Paul, "A Structured Family Interview," *Family Process*, vol. 5, no. 2 (September, 1956), pp. 256–271.

———, J. Beavin, and D. Jackson, *Pragmatics of Human Communication* (New York: Norton, 1967).

Whitaker, Carl, Workshop, Pine Manor Junior College, Brookline, Mass.: Human Resources Institute, April 19, 1974.

———, and Janet Burdy, "Family Psychotherapy of a Psychopathic Personality: Must Every Member Change?" *Comprehensive Psychiatry*, vol. 10, no. 5 (September, 1969), pp. 361–364.

———, Thomas P. Malone, and John Warkentin, "Multiple Therapy and Psychotherapy," reprint from *Progress in Psychotherapy* (New York: Grune & Stratton, 1956).

OTHER CONTEMPORARY THERAPIES AND THEORIES

Agel, Jerome, et al., *The Radical Therapist* (New York: Ballantine Books, 1971).

Bateson, Gregory, *Steps to an Ecology of Mind* (New York: Ballantine Books, 1972).

Berne, Eric, *Games People Play* (New York: Dell, 1964).

———, *What Do You Say After You Say Hello?* (New York: Bantam Books, 1973).

Branden, Nathaniel, *The Disowned Self* (Los Angeles, Calif.: Nash Publishing Co., 1971).

———, *The Psychology of Self-Esteem* (Los Angeles, Calif.: Nash Publishing Co., 1969).

Goffman, Irving, *Strategic Interaction* (New York: Ballantine Books, 1969).

Halleck, Seymour L., *The Politics of Therapy* (New York: Science House, 1971).

Harris, Thomas A., *I'm OK, You're OK: A Practical Guide to Transactional Analysis* (New York: Harper & Row, 1969).

Janov, Arthur, *The Primal Revolution* (New York: Simon & Schuster, 1972).

———, *The Primal Scream* (New York: Dell, 1970).

Karlins, Marvin, and Lewis M. Andrews, *Biofeedback* (Philadelphia: Lippincott, 1972).

Mack, John, *Nightmares and Human Conflict* (Boston: Houghton Mifflin, 1974).

Maslow, Abraham H., *Toward a Psychology of Being* (New York: Van Nostrand Reinhold, 1968).

May, Rollo, *The Art of Counseling* (Nashville, Tenn.: Abingdon, 1967).

Perls, Frederick, *Gestalt Therapy Verbatim* (Lafayette, Calif.: Real People Press, 1969).
――――, Ralph Hefferline, and Paul Goodman, *Gestalt Therapy* (New York: Julian Messner, 1951).
Schutz, William C., *Joy* (New York: Grove Press, 1967).
――――, *Here Comes Everybody* (New York: Harper & Row, 1971).
Szasz, Thomas S., *The Myth of Mental Illness* (New York: Dell, 1961)
Yablonsky, Lewis, *Synanon: The Tunnel Back* (Baltimore: Penguin Books, 1967).

SEX

Goldstein, Martin, et al, *The Sex Book* (New York: Herder & Herder, 1971).
Hamilton, Eleanor, *Sex Before Marriage* (New York: Hawthorne Press, 1969).
――――, Workshop, Cape Breton Island, Nova Scotia: "Sex Counseling, Process and Techniques," sponsored by Hamilton School Counseling Center, Sheffield, Mass., June 17–28, 1974.
Kaplan, Helen Singer, *The New Sex Therapy* (New York: Brunner/Mazel, 1974).
Kinsey, Alfred C., *Sexual Behavior in the Human Female* (Philadelphia: W. B. Saunders, 1953).
――――, *Sexual Behavior in the Human Male* (Philadelphia: W. B. Saunders, 1948).
Reuben, David, *Everything You Always Wanted to Know About Sex but Were Afraid to Ask* (New York: David McKay Co., 1969).
Rosenberg, Jack Lee, *Total Orgasm* (New York and Berkeley, Calif.: Random House and Bookworks, 1973).
Rush, Anne Kent, *Getting Clear* (New York: Random House, 1973).
――――, *Our Bodies, Ourselves* (New York: Random House, 1972).
Selzer, Joae Graham, *When Children Ask about Sex* (Boston: Beacon Press, 1974).
Wyden, Peter, and Barbara Wyden, *A Candid Inquiry inside the Sex Clinic* (Cleveland: World Publishing, 1971).

SEXISM

Chesler, Phyllis, *Women and Madness* (New York: Doubleday, 1972).
Daly, Mary, *Beyond God the Father* (Boston: Beacon Press, 1973).
de Beauvoir, Simone, *The Second Sex* (New York: Knopf, 1952).
Greer, Germaine, *The Female Eunuch* (New York: McGraw-Hill, 1970).
Millet, Kate, *The Prostitution Papers* (New York: Basic Books, 1971).
――――, *Sexual Politics* (New York: Doubleday, 1969).
Mitchell, Juliet, *Psychoanalysis and Feminism* (New York: Random House, 1974).